WRITERS AND SOCIETY IN MODERN JAPAN

WRITERS AND SOCIETY IN MODERN JAPAN

Irena Powell

KODANSHA INTERNATIONAL LTD.
Tokyo, New York and San Francisco

First published 1983 by
THE MACMILLAN PRESS LTD
London and Basingstoke
Companies and representatives
throughout the world

First published in Japan and the USA 1983 by
KODANSHA INTERNATIONAL LTD.
12–21, Otowa 2-chome, Bunkyo-ku, Tokyo 112 and
KODANSHA INTERNATIONAL/USA LTD.
10 East 53rd Street, New York, N.Y. 10022
and 44 Montgomery Street, San Francisco,
California 94104

LCC 82-48432
ISBN 0-87011-558-8
ISBN 4-7700-1042-7 (in Japan)

Printed in Hong Kong

To Mayama Miho sensei
without whose generous help and understanding
this book would have never been written

Contents

Acknowledgement

I should like to express my warmest thanks to my husband Brian Powell who supervised this work when it was still at its thesis stage, and who later gave me his full support throughout the lengthy process of rewriting the thesis into a book.

Every effort has been made to trace all the copyright-holders, but if any have been inadvertently overlooked, the publishers will be pleased to make the necessary arrangements at the first opportunity.

I. P.

Introduction

Modern Japanese literature has increasingly attracted the attention of scholars over the past decade, but in spite of this it still remains an area largely unknown to the Western reader. Those who out of curiosity or interest struggle through the available translations are often left wondering about the meaning of the work or the intentions of the author. They are struck by the strangeness of unfamiliar issues, the odd solutions to conflicts or even the complete absence of such solutions. The plot is slack and undramatic, and there is a puzzling lack of 'real' issues, which often seem to have been replaced by abundant imagery of an erotic or aesthetic nature. Such readers seldom find their expectations, nurtured on Western literary taste, at all satisfied. They do not derive the enjoyment expected from the act of reading a work of literature, nor do they, if that indeed was their original aim, increase significantly their knowledge about Japan.

The degree of difficulty experienced by the Western reader in appreciating modern Japanese literature suggests perhaps a need for a frame of reference. This might enable him to increase his level of comprehension and add to the pleasure and enjoyment that an encounter with the unfamiliar world of the Japanese novel would bring. This should provide him not only with specific information about the intrinsic development of modern Japanese literature, but also with a general picture of the cultural and social context in which such development took place. It is within the latter part of this proposition, in the extrinsic approach which examines the relationship between literature and society, that this book hopes to make a contribution towards a better understanding of the major themes and pre-occupations of modern Japanese literature. The purpose of this book is to seek some social explanations for the phenomenon of modern Japanese literature, to examine its environment and the forces which formed it.

One reservation should perhaps be made here: that no single

relation is sought for as linking works of art on the one hand and
social and cultural conditions on the other. No claim is made for
exclusive validity in the following sociological explanation of art.
The method is applied to demonstrate the various extra-literary
influences which may be exerted on literature while avoiding the
dogmatism of economic determinism.

A sociological approach in literary studies is usually based on two
major assumptions: first, that literary development derives *not only*
from the internal momentum of the literary tradition and, secondly,
that literature is an aspect of society and, in a particular sense, a
social institution around which traditions, customs and patterns of
behaviour have come together. Literature lacks the firm structure of
political, legal or religious institutions, but it has a distinct network
of relations and processes (some of which will be discussed in this
book) which make it possible to speak about it as an institution and
to study it as such.[1]

The sociology of literature is generally divided into three main
areas: the sociology of the writer, the social content of the literary
works themselves, and the influence of literature on society.[2] This
study will confine itself to the sociology of the writer, as it is here that
the main discussion of literary institutions and of the profession of
writing takes place. The sociology of the writer covers a wide
spectrum of subjects: the writers, their socialisation and training,
their roles, careers and modes of creativity; the distribution and
reward system, including patrons and publishers; critics with their
typical outlets, forms of expression and their professional
associations; and finally the public.

It may involve certain models which are part of the Marxist
inheritance. George Huaco, an American sociologist, suggests that
literary phenomena are surrounded by what he calls the five social
structures:

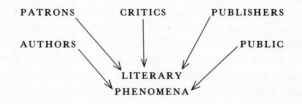

He also maintains, however, that any relevant analysis of a
historically specific matrix of art or literature has to refer the above

and similar 'medium range' models to a larger one which analyses the major political, social and economic changes in the larger society. The formal link between the two models is the assumption that major changes in the larger society tend to affect art, literature or film, by being channelled through the social structures.[3]

The sociological approach offers a perspective through which a study of the literary milieu can be conducted. Rather than involve itself in the individual life histories of particular writers, it leads to a presentation of writers as types at a particular time in a particular society. The whole economic basis of writing – the milieu from which the writers came and in which they lived, the social status of the writers, the literary associations, the degree of integration in social processes, the relationship with the audience – these are the elements of this typological characterisation. Of these, the social origin of the writer plays only a minor part in defining his social affiliation. Throughout history writers were men who, through their insight and education, were able to free themselves from the class into which they had been born, and ally themselves intellectually with other strata of society. In modern times in particular, they form a semi-independent, in-between class or social group, to which Mannheim's definition of 'free' intellectuals seems to be more appropriate. The social characteristics of the professional group of which he is a member are of considerably more relevance in discussing the modern writer.

The following discussion of the social context of modern Japanese literature will concentrate on the emergence and development of the modern professional literary milieu, usually referred to in Japanese critical literature as the *bundan*, in a historical perspective, from the time when the modernisation of the country began in the late nineteenth century until the collapse of Imperial Japan at the end of the Second World War. The periodisation adopted will follow the Japanese convention of applying historical divisions to literary development; hence we talk about the Meiji (1868–1912), Taishō (1912–26) and Shōwa (1926–) *bundan*. It should also be mentioned that the way in which the term *bundan* is used in Japanese literary criticism implies the existence of at least two definitions of the *bundan* itself: the one wide in scope, which includes most people involved in literary activities and comes close perhaps to the English notion of the 'literary world' or 'literary establishment'; and the other narrower, referring mainly to the small community of creative writers engaged in serious, so-called 'pure' literature, which can be perhaps rendered into English as 'literary élite'. Not all the serious writers were necessarily at all times members of the *bundan* in the narrow definition. Some were repelled by the *bundan*'s attitudes and preferred to stay outside. It was the narrow *bundan* – the exclusive, sectarian community of professional writers – that had a profound influence on the development and character of Japanese literature in the twentieth century. The main literary currents will be presented in this study, in chronological order, through the perspective of the internal divisions and developments in the *bundan*.

It is hoped that by examining the modes of thought and behaviour of Japanese writers in the *bundan*, patterns will emerge which will indicate the close relationship between the artist's vision of the world as expressed in his creative works, and the social and historical reality of his *bundan* life. As the sociologist L. Goldmann has shown, such patterns do not belong to either the realm of literature or that of society, but form an important, meaningful link between the two. They tend to ignore the existence of the individual writer in favour of a typological characteristic of a group or generation:

> The essential relationship between the life of society and literary creation is not concerned with the content of these two sectors of human reality, but only with the mental structures, which might be called the categories which shape both the empirical consciousness of a certain social group and the imaginary universe created by the writer.
>
> The experience of a single individual is much too brief and too limited to be able to create such mental structure; this can only be the result of the conjoint activity of a large number of individuals who find themselves in a similar situation, that is to say, who constitute a privileged social group, these individuals having, for a lengthy period and in an intensive way, lived through a series of problems and having endeavoured to find a significant solution to them. This means that mental structures or, to use a more abstract term, significant categorical structures, are not individual phenomena, but social phenomena.[4]

Looking through Japanese critical literature one finds re-markably little material bearing directly on the subject of the *bundan* as a social phenomenon. The market is flooded by detailed biographical studies emphasising the personality of the artist, histories of literary movements based on internal developments or sometimes within the context of the historical circumstances of the nation. There is also a surprising number of personal accounts and reminiscences based on encounters, friendships or business dealings with famous authors. Such sources, when used with care, may at best provide limited information about the social environment of literature, once the overall model has been formed.

In the search for general structures of literary behaviour in Japan it may perhaps be useful to turn to the immediate post-war period in Japanese literary criticism, when in the atmosphere of a newly-acquired freedom of expression a thorough re-examination of the old value system, including the purpose, character and role of literature, took place. Underlying the need for this re-examination were the guilt feelings of Japanese intellectuals who accused themselves of failing to provide a significant opposition to the totalitarian military regime of the 1930s, which led the nation into war.

The extensive literary discussion that developed in the literary columns of newspapers and magazines during the first post-war decade concentrated on two large issues:

1. The mutual relation between literature and politics, and literature and society – a continuation of the pre-war dialogue between Marxist and non-Marxist literature.[5]
2. The need to create a national literature as opposed to the self-centred, narrow form of *watakushi shōsetsu* (autobiographical novel) which had reigned supreme in the literary world for the previous half century.[6]

Underlying both problems was the question of the role of the *bundan* and the significance of the part which it played in the development of modern Japanese literature.

The discussion was dominated by such giants of modern literary criticism as Itō Sei, Hirano Ken, Nakamura Mitsuo, Ara Masahito, Fukuda Tsuneari and Honda Shūgo, whose contributions subsequently formed the core of Japanese studies on modern Japanese literature. They belonged to the pre-war generation and their views are of particular interest as they experienced themselves in their own lives the vicissitudes, traumas and dilemmas of the pre-war *bundan*. In their youth they had been exposed to the violent impact of the Marxist literary movement which had put the established *bundan* writers on the defensive. Some of them, like Itō Sei, Nakamura Mitsuo and Fukuda Tsuneari defended the *bundan*'s view of art, whereas others went through a period of alignment with the left-wing movement. There had followed the ruthless State suppression of all radical and liberal thought in the 1930s during the so-called 'dark valley' period of Japanese history, when most writers were forced either into a 'conversion' from radical thought and silence or into overt support for the nationalistic and expansionist policies of the State. The post-war 'democratic revolution', as it is sometimes referred to by Japanese historians, in spite of the fact that it was enforced from above by a foreign occupation power, created a long-awaited opportunity for a new and open examination of the whole history of Japanese literature. In the soul-searching mood of the period, which demanded an answer to the question of what went wrong, criticism was predominantly directed against the pre-war *bundan*. The detailed scrutiny of the pre-war *bundan* that took place in the first decade after the war constitutes the main source material for this study. It will be presented here in preference to the ideas and opinions expressed by the next, the so-called post-war generation, which matured during the war and emerged on the literary scene in the post-war period. Being of a different generation they were able to view the literary past of their country and the lives of their predecessors with more detachment and objectivity. Their writings opened a new chapter in Japanese literary criticism and they are of vital importance to anyone interested in modern Japanese literature. However, they merit much fuller treatment than would be possible in the present volume and should form the subject of a separate study if one is going to do justice to the sheer size and diversity of their output.

Consequently, this book sets out to present the theories, formulated mainly by critics of the pre-war generation, concerning patterns of thought and behaviour in the *bundan*, the estrangement of the latter from the life of the nation, and its influence on modern Japanese literature.

Proportionately most space, however, will be devoted to the ideas expounded by the poet, novelist and critic, Itō Sei (1905–69). The originality of his views, the comprehensiveness of his approach, and his tireless search for the basic structures that have shaped modern Japanese literature, deserve special attention. The literary terminology which he invented has entered the stock vocabulary of Japanese literary scholarship, and no discussion of the *bundan*, in present-day Japan, fails to mention his views. His position within the *bundan* was a curious one. He came to Tokyo as a young man from the northern island of Hokkaido, neither a graduate of a famous university nor a disciple of a famous writer. To the end of his life, in spite of the recognition accorded to him by the *bundan*, he preserved a feeling of being an outsider which gave his observations of the *bundan* some detachment and additional sharpness. Combined with his first-hand knowledge of the mechanisms through which the *bundan* operated, this produced unusually informative works about the professional literary world which no outsider could ever hope to penetrate and which no inside member of the *bundan* was perhaps capable of describing with an equally critical eye.

Itō Sei's theories were often criticised in later years for creating a picture of the *bundan* which did not entirely correspond to reality, for getting some of the facts wrong, for overemphasising the Meiji and Taishō periods as shaping the character of modern Japanese literature, and for underestimating the dramatic events of the Shōwa period.[7] He has, however, no successor. We must wait for someone who can combine his breadth of vision with modern knowledge of the theory and sociology of literature, to present a similarly comprehensive account of the Japanese literary world. So far, it is still mostly Itō Sei's work to which the reader goes when seeking an insight into the factors that shaped the mentality of modern Japanese writers.

1 The Meiji Literary World: the Struggle for Modernisation

INTRODUCTION

To establish the process by which the literary world of early Meiji Japan,[1] inherited from the Tokugawa period (1615–1868), was transformed into one which may be called 'modern', it is useful to accept the organising concept of Japan as a country undergoing the process of modernisation. Modernisation, according to J. Hall, 'involves the systematic, sustained and purposeful application of human energies to the *rational* [author's italics] control of man's physical and social environment for various human purposes'.[2] It is within the context of the battle between the irrational and rational elements in the patterns of thought and behaviour of Japanese writers that the modernisation of Japanese literature took place. In its background lies the gradual process of transformation of the whole country from a pre-modern type of society into a modern state.

One of the basic features of modernisation is an increase in the value placed upon the individual. In a traditional society which is relatively homogeneous in its beliefs and values and is typically rural rather than urban, men tend to function through traditional status arrangements. They live by certain willing renunciations and by ideologies that encourage them to adjust to their lot, restrain excessive aspiration, and fulfil themselves through inherited roles, patterns of conduct and a cohesive sense of community. Modern society, which is typically urban or at least city-orientated, encourages social mobility and offers its members a variety of roles and status. Men have greater opportunity for independent selfhood as they depend on a multiplicity of relationships. They live in a world

1

in which self-definition seems more possible, and they stress ideologies emphasising opportunity, freedom, liberation, independence and self-completion.[3] This finds its reflection in the world of literature, where the balance maintained between man and the social processes around him becomes the recurrent intellectual and emotional theme of our era.

Japanese literary historians generally agree that the rise of individualism – the subjective, individualist and private orientation of life and literature which has taken place in the last two hundred years in Europe, occurred in Japan only at the beginning of this century, when the so-called 'naturalist' writers emerged on the literary scene, i.e. almost forty years after the process of modernisation of the country had started.

If we accept these forty years as a transition period for the Japanese literary establishment in its progress towards modernity, our first task will be to consider the problems which exercised the attention of writers in Japanese society during that period, especially those which had a bearing on the character of the literary world and the literature produced by it. We will observe how the impact of modernisation created favourable conditions for a change in the status of novelist and novels in the new Meiji Japan, and how this change affected the way of life of the members of the first professional literary groups, who found themselves confronted with the traditional social structure on the one hand and new patterns of life emerging under the influence of the modernisation effort on the other. And last, but not least, we will observe the diminishing degree of social integration and participation of writers, which at the end of the forty-year period led to their withdrawal into a community of their own, the *bundan*.

THE TOKUGAWA HERITAGE

To appreciate the changes which took place after the Meiji Restoration, both in the types of literature and the status of the writers, one has to remember that in Tokugawa Japan (1615–1868) there existed two separate, almost mutually exclusive, worlds of letters:

1. That of pure literature, written in Chinese or *kanbuncho* by educated *samurai*, scholars, court officials or poets for the consumption of the intellectual elite.

2. That of popular literature: novels, humorous stories, sentimental love adventures and didactic stories, full of mysterious
occurrences, encouraging virtue and chastising vice (*kanzen
chōaku*), composed in a curious mixture of formal and
colloquial language, written for the entertainment of the
lower classes, and considered by intellectuals to be crude and
vulgar, only suitable for women and children.[4]

The generic term customarily used to describe the popular fiction
of the Tokugawa period is *gesaku*, a playful composition in D.
Keene's translation. According to Keene the term was first used by
the *samurai* Hirata Gennai (1729–79) to distinguish his serious
writings from his works of popular literature which he qualified as
gesaku.'The word "playful" referred not to the subject matter of his
drama – historical tragedy – but to the professed attitude of the
author. By preserving a suitable distance from his own creation,
Gennai adopted the stance of the dilettante who disclaims responsibility for a composition he never intended seriously.'[5] Although
members of the educated élite were officially discouraged from
reading or writing *gesaku*, nevertheless it often provided an outlet for
the frustrated energies of the cultivated men and authors of *samurai*
origin.

The social status of the professional *gesaku* writer was very low.
Together with geisha and actors, novelists were considered to
belong to the *demi-monde* of popular entertainers. Theatre, art and
literature living in close contact with the licenced quarters (which
often consituted the subject of *gesaku* fiction) created in the
Tokugawa period a world of popular culture which was anti-
establishment in spirit. The frivolous nature of the *gesaku* literature
was frowned upon by the Confucian establishment and the
writers often fell victim to the publication laws, their freedom
being temporarily restricted and their books banned or con-
fiscated.

Low manuscript fees (generally authors sold the complete rights
to the publishers without any royalties)[6] formed another aspect of
the precarious existence of these writers. Only the most successful
ones were able to establish themselves professionally and make their
living by writing. Others were forced to take employment, run
businesses or seek other sources of livelihood. For instance, Kanagaki Robun (1829–94), a very popular writer of the late
Tokugawa and early Meiji periods, earned his living first as a writer

of letters and commercial advertisements,[7] and later as the manager of a second-hand furniture store and pharmacy.

Another source of income (common at the time to writers and artists alike) was the favour of a rich town merchant whom the writer would accompany on trips to the gay quarters and the theatre, and for whose benefit he would compose comic songs and poems. In this context, the writer was no more than a professional jester entertaining his master, for which services he was rewarded with small sums of money and presents in kind such as *kimono*, tobacco holders, etc. Thus the merchant would act as a kind of literary patron offering the writer some financial support.[8]

At the bottom of the social ladder, caught between the watchful eye of officialdom and economic insecurity, the writers led a very uncertain existence. Although the situation changed considerably in Meiji Japan and the modern writers approached literature with the intensity of purpose that made them treat themselves much more seriously, neverthless the 'outlaw' mentality inherited from the Edo period was never far from the surface, ready to manifest itself when the circumstances changed again.

THE AGE OF ENLIGHTENMENT

The first twenty years of the Meiji period are often referred to by Japanese and Western scholars as 'a period of civilisation and enlightenment'.[9] During this time the main role belonged to the men of knowledge, for whom the government, which aimed at transforming Japan into a militarily strong, modern nation, had a great use and need. The intellectual mission was to enlighten the people and the government so that they would understand Western science and institute national reforms along European lines. The battle was fought on all fronts, everything was a subject for discussion from politics, business and law to social mores, ways of living, eating and dressing.

One of the main topics under discussion was the language itself. If the people were to be educated to work for the advancement of their country, they had to understand the language which newspapers, textbooks and magazines were using. In the call for language reform reference was frequently made to the unity of speech and writing in Western countries. It was argued that Japan would never be able to take its place among the advanced nations of the world until her written and spoken languages were merged. As a result of this widespread discussion, by the late 1870s there was a strong tendency among scholars, educators and journalists to abandon the Chinese or *kanbunchō* style in favour of a relatively straightforward prose closely approximating the spoken language.[10]

The main forum for discussing the issue of the day was the fast developing selection of daily newspapers and weekly magazines, whose editors and contributors were usually highly learned men with advanced political views. Many of them were ex-*samurai* of the non-conforming type, who were unwilling to serve the clan coalition which made up the Meiji government, and they made journalism into an enclave of free opposition to the government.

For talented novelists and literary men of the late Tokugawa period, who after the Restoration faced the problem of how to make a living from writing, newspapers presented a new, ideal opportunity for advance in the world. Kanagaki Robun joined the staff of the Yokohama *Mainichi Shinbun* (the first daily newspaper in modern Japan) in 1871 and his career set a pattern followed by most *gesaku* novelists at the time. Newspapers offered their employees a regular income in return for daily reports, and they gradually opened their columns to serialised novels. At the beginning, the latter were simply fictionalised narratives of events which had first been reported as news items in the social columns. This was the origin of the so-called 'newspaper novel' which enjoys an undiminishing popularity to this day. The process by which an article on social affairs was transformed into a novel was not dissimilar to the way in which great writers of the pre-modern era such as Chikamatsu Monzaemon and Ihara Saikaku dramatised in their works the events that constituted news in their time (for example, conflagrations, love suicides and murders).

The writers turned to newspapers to earn their living and find an opportunity to publish. An aspiring novelist would seek the patronage of a leading writer on one of the papers and then join the paper through the latter's recommendation. Once there he had to go through a period of journalistic apprenticeship and only after his talent had been acknowledged was he allowed the privilege of serialising his own novels. One could not, in fact, survive as a writer in those early years of Meiji without holding a newspaper or magazine post, and it was a general rule at the time that writers wrote exclusively for the papers by which they were employed.[11]

In the course of time a natural rift appeared between the so-called 'small' popular press where most *gesaku* novelists published their works, and the serious press of a more political and polemic orientation. The latter soon fell victim to State oppression. The anti-press laws of 1875 closed down several newspapers and resulted in the arrests of many prominent journalists. This government action produced a counter-effect, however, in hastening the emergence of the political novel, a new genre written by those writers who could no longer write political articles. The political novels postulated in a camouflaged, allegorical way the political demands of the popular rights movement of the 1880s for the promulgation of a constitution. They had a purely utilitarian purpose and value, and disappeared when the Meiji Constitution was promulgated and the first Diet established (1889 and 1890).

Thus for almost two decades the Meiji period failed to produce any works of outstanding literary value, the nation being pre-occupied with the task of creating the foundations for a modern State. All writers were journalists, and while some continued to write rather mediocre Tokugawa-type popular literature for entertainment, others welcomed the chance of participation in the complicated but exciting political issues of their time. At the end of this period, new factors appeared:

1. There emerged, as a result of the Meiji educational reforms, an educated public which wished to read books, and a rapid extension of the publishing business followed to answer its demands. This in turn fostered the professionalisation of writing as it widened the marketing opportunities for works of literature.
2. A new generation of young novelists, educated at the new universities established after the Restoration, and often referred to as the 'new Meiji generation' began to assume a prominent position in the world of letters. These writers, in spite of their youth (they were all in their early twenties), brought new ideas into the vacuum that existed in the world of literature.

MEIJI YOUTH

The expression 'Meiji youth' was first used by a journalist, Tokutomi Sohō (1863–1957), who was a member of that generation himself and its main spokesman,[12] while his younger brother, the novelist Tokutomi Roka (1868–1927), related the life history of someone who might be considered a typical Meiji youth, in his largely autobiographical work *Omoide no ki* (A Record of Memories, 1901).[13]

The term refers to Japanese born around the time of the Meiji Restoration who until their teens received traditional training at home and in private academies and then, following their own wishes, pursued their education in the newly-established schools, where they were 'taught by Western instructors, tutored in freshly translated texts and proselytised by newly arrived missionaries'.[14] Graduates of these schools entered society with a passionate belief in the idea of the independence and self-determination of the individual, and a strong conviction that it was the democratic right of every individual, regardless of his status or class, to be able to attain a high position solely on the basis of his ability and merit. For those young people, writes Professor Maruyama Masao, who 'had only recently emerged from the stagnant atmosphere of an isolated country, and found themselves freed from the suffocating hierarchies of social status', the idea of advancement in life was a compelling one, and education was the means by which they could fulfil their aspirations.[15]

For instance, in 1885 in the preparatory course of Tokyo Imperial University were writers such as Natsume Sōseki, Yamada Bimyō, Masaoka Shiki, Ozaki Kōyō, Kawakami Bizan and Ishibashi Shian. Mori Ōgai and Tsubouchi Shōyō had graduated from the same university, respectively, only four and two years earlier. Later, when Tsubouchi, who lectured at Waseda University (at the time named Tokyo Senmon Gakkō), became famous for his studies of modern literature and his Shakespeare translations, students with literary interests drifted towards Waseda University, a tendency which exists even today. Many of these young people never finished the courses which they started, but the university friendships which they made remained an important factor in forming literary groups. They constituted the cultural elite of the nation, and as such contributed greatly to the rise in the social status of writer. They all came to live in Tokyo, which was the symbol of everything new in Meiji Japan. It was an environment generating new values, new thought and new art, where intellectual excitement was linked with new possibilities for independence, and where a writer could find a new role for himself.

The world of newspapers and magazines in which most of the young intelligentsia found employment, offered them a new freedom and a chance for success and fame outside the restrictive social system, as it had few connections with the established academic, bureaucratic, business and military cliques. In the late 1880s and the 1890s journalists and writers formed within this world a semi-independent community which became known as the Meiji *bundan*. This was a social unit which exerted a certain type of cultural influence and came to be one of the main features of the Meiji intellectual scene.

THE MEIJI *BUNDAN*

The nucleus of the Meiji *bundan* was formed when a young writer, Ozaki Kōyō (1867–1903), founded in 1885 a literary society called *Ken'yūsha* (Friends of the Inkstone). The society started its activities by publishing a magazine *Garakuta bunko* (Literary Odds and Ends), which was the first of its kind and set a pattern for future private coterie magazines published by small literary groups. It was clear from the very first number of the journal that the members of *Ken'yūsha* intended to treat literature not as a hobby but as a vocation and profession, ensuring the demand for their works by appealing to a wide range of readers. The very fact of editing a journal was a conscious attempt on the part of this group of writers at self-determination, at defining the purpose of literature and the role of the writer in the new Japan. It was a declaration of strength and of the independence of the literary profession.

The views on literature held by the members of the *Ken'yūsha* group were, in fact, not very precise. They felt attracted to the new ideas of psychological truth and realism in literature postulated by Tsubouchi Shōyō in the theoretical essay *Shōsetsu shinzui* (The Essence of the Novel), which appeared in the same year in which *Ken'yūsha* was founded. Above all, however, they believed in the entertainment value of literature and continued to write sentimental love stories in the traditional vein. In contrast to late Tokugawa fiction, Kōyō's works were beautifully written literary masterpieces. In addition, their main theme of love had changed its connotation under Western and Christian influence; it was now no longer an expression of immoral libertinism but of innate humanity, and this gave the works a new depth. The *Ken'yūsha* writers established themselves and gained recognition through the aesthetic and entertaining qualities of their works, ignoring almost completely the social, political and spiritual upheavals of their time. By portraying characters whose lives were frustrated by outmoded ethical values, they appealed to readers who, twenty years after the Meiji Restoration, still found themselves bound to the old, feudal ways of life through their family ties or places of work. The classic literary style with which these novelists sought to appeal to the taste of their readers evolved from the *gesaku* tradition, and reflected the emotional formalism of Meiji society, where the remnants of Tokugawa feudalism combined with the absolutist aspirations of the modern State to impede the rapid development of individual freedom.

In 1889 Ozaki Kōyō published *Ninin bikuni iro zange* (The Amorous Confessions of Two Nuns), a novel about the suffering of lovers in feudal times. The beautiful style of this work established the author as the most important novelist of the post-Restoration period, and secured him, at the age of twenty-three, a post of literary editor with the *Yomiuri shinbun*. With its circulation of 30,000 this newspaper was the largest and the most influential in Tokyo. Retention of a talented novelist by a newspaper in this way was designed to improve the quality of the literary works appearing in its pages. The system continued throughout the Meiji and, to a lesser extent, the Taishō periods. In exchange, writers like Kōyō exerted great influence on literary policy. When Kōyō became a staff member of *Yomiuri shinbun*, he and his followers found there an open forum for their works. In addition, their works began appearing in book form. Publication of a series entitled *Shinchō hyaku shū* (Hundred Novels by New Authors) was commenced by the publishing house Yoshioka Shoten, and the first volume contained Kōyō's *Iro zange*. Kōyō himself subsequently became an editor of the series. The same publishing house later sponsored the society's organ *Garakuta bunko*.

A contemporary critic, quoted by Tsubouchi Shōyō in his introduction to *Iro zange*, describes Kōyō and his group as the 'operational centre of the *bundan*'. This was the first time the word '*bundan*' had been used in the context of modern Japanese literature, and the way in which it was used indicated that a new phenomenon was developing in the literary life of the country. The *Ken'yūsha* writers established new patterns of *modus operandi* or even *modus vivendi* of writers in society. They no longer belonged to the *demi-*

monde of courtesans, geisha and actors. They were a group of writers conscious of their artistic mission, powerful enough to enforce their own standards of literary taste and able, through the stronghold which they had founded in publishing and journalism, to defend their own interests.

The style of life of these professional 'journalists *cum* novelists' of the mid-Meiji period often offended the mores of respectable society. Sake drinking, affairs with women, and unsettled family lives were of common occurrence and came to be considered by the general public almost as a professional hazard of the writer.

Ironically perhaps, in spite of their unconventional, or as the writers themselves saw it, their free way of life, the pattern of relationships within their own community resembled very closely the social structures of the outside world which they were so anxious to leave. What united the *Ken'yūsha* writers, apart from the vague notion of becoming good writers, were personal connections of friendships, the teacher–student type of relationship, feelings of duty and obligation, etc., in other words the set of attitudes typical of any social institution in Japan.

SOCIAL STRUCTURE

Ken'yūsha, in its approach to writing as a profession and in the control which it had over the literary market, reminds one of the era of professional guilds in Europe, which exercised considerable control over the arts, both in terms of the number of recruits and the course of their careers. For instance, the disciples had to remain with the master for a certain defined number of years, and they could not change masters unless their first teacher agreed to break the contract. But while the rules of medieval guilds were dictated by the need to protect the profession against competition in a free market, the guild-like relations within the Meiji *bundan* had their roots in the traditional Japanese social structure.

The most conspicuous traditional pattern of organisation that survived among the artists and scholars from the pre-modern era was the so-called apprenticeship system (*totei seidō*), based on a vertical relationship between the master and his disciples.[16]

There is a description of what such a relationship entailed in the book *Japanese Society* by Chie Nakane:

Social recognition of one's proficiency derives from the link with one's teacher, rather than from free competition. This system tends to blur the difference in individual merit, since once a personal relation is established between a teacher and a student, the teacher seldom dismisses his student, because it is considered that the greater the number of students, the greater the teacher's prestige as well as his income. Students under one teacher compete with each other to get their teacher's favour – that is the only way for them to acquire fame – for which they often employ other means than proficiency in art. Therefore a man who is really talented and has achieved proficiency may fail in his career owing to his bad relations with his teacher and colleagues as well as the relative weakness of the group to which the teacher belongs, in comparison with other competing groups. Moreover, in this system he may be greatly handicapped in training, because he is not able to approach teachers in other areas or groups. Although such an action is possible theoretically, it entails an obvious loss for him, since it invites general suspicion of his loyalty to his teacher, and may well entail loss of his teacher's favour.[17]

The apprenticeship system provided a specific social context for the development of modern literature: the possibility of a free market was hindered from the start by the protectionalism and practice of patronage which existed within the literary world.

The old traditional term *mon*, meaning school or receiving education under the master, was used by contemporaries in reference to Kōyō's establishment, and his associates were referred to as Kōyō *monka* or *monkasei*, i.e. disciples, those studying under Kōyō. The traditional order of relations between the master and his pupil friends was preserved here.

A particular category of students or followers comprised those who lived in the master's house (*shosei*). It was a common practice at the time for a scholar, politician or man of letters to take one or two potential successors into his home and, while using them as assistants or servants, to train them in their profession.

For instance, at Kōyō's house there were at different periods of time four to eight *shosei*.[18] Of them all Izumi Kyōka and Oguri Fūyō were the most assiduous students of the classic type and the most faithful followers of Kōyō's instruction. They were consequently the best loved and best cared for by the teacher, and under his direct guidance they advanced the most rapidly.[19] Similarly, at the house of Tsubouchi Shōyō lived Yazaki Saganoya, and also, for a short time during his literary career, Futabatei Shimei.

The teacher's role was to provide the *shosei* with board, lodging and clothes. He also examined his lodger's work, corrected and gave advice on it, and arranged for him to publish it. The *shosei's* work was often published under the teacher's name or under the joint names of both of them. This was intended to help the sales, as works by totally unknown authors could not be expected to attract the attention which was given to those by established authors. Money received from publishers in such cases was often shared. This was the case with Futabatei's *Ukigumo*, which was first published under Tsubouchi's name. Tsubouchi handed over part of the fees received from the publisher to Futabatei. This was also the cause of the quarrel and eventual break of the master–student relationship between Hirotsu Ryūrō and Nagai Kafū, as the former used to spend the money which he received from publishers in Tokyo bars.[20]

This type of relationship between writers in Meiji Japan may be better understood if it is seen in the context of the traditional Japanese *oyabun–kobun* relation, which again is a relation between two individuals of upper and lower status. *Oya* means a person with the status of a parent and *kobun* means one with the status of child. The traditional *oyabun–kobun* relationship took the form of patron and client, land-owner and tenant, or for instance, master and disciple. The essential elements in the relationship are that the *kobun* receives benefits or help from his *oyabun*, such as assistance in securing employment or promotion, or advice on the occasion of important decision-making. The *kobun*, in turn, is ready to offer his services whenever the *oyabun* requires them.[21] In view of the traditional elements preserved within the social structure of the literary world, Itō Sei wrote: 'The Meiji *bundan* was a small, half-feudal literary establishment, in which young writers were supposed to learn not only how to write, but also how to live.'[22]

But in spite of its 'traditionalism', the *bundan* performed the important function of providing an intellectual community to the previously isolated men of letters. A young person who arrived in Tokyo from the country with dreams of making a literary career, was provided inside the *bundan* with an opportunity of gaining an independent existence as an artist. He was also provided with a circle of people to whom he could address himself and who bestowed their recognition. In this respect the *bundan* played a role similar to that played in Europe by the literary salons of seventeenth- and eighteenth-century France, the London coffee houses of the age of Addison, and the literary clubs of the age of Johnson, where men of letters had an opportunity to meet their fellow writers.

Tokyo's literary life in the 1880s, lively as it was in a period which abounded with young prolific writers, concentrated round small *sushi* bars, where writers spent their time drinking sake, gossiping, and discussing professional matters. But the basic structure of the *bundan*, which was split into a number of schools (of which the most powerful was the *Kōyō-mon*) each united under the authority of a master with strong vertical teacher–student ties, separated the writers into small groups or school-cliques (*monbatsu*), as their critics called them, which had little contact with one another. Each had its own favourite place of meeting, its own faithful followers and its own contacts with the publishing business, and each supported its own members.[23]

This socio-cultural pattern of small, exclusive groups with poor inter-group relations and communication and a strongly hierarchical internal structure is not by any means limited to the literary world. The same situation can be found among journalists, artists, musicians or professional academics, thus hindering the full development of those fields where the nature of the work ideally demands free competition.

The phenomenon was described by Maruyama Masao as *takotsubo*, or octopus-trap formation, referring to the way in which identical traps stand in a row, completely isolated from each other and each constructed in such a way that there is no escape. He compared this typically Japanese structure to the one predominant in Europe which he described as *sasara*, a bamboo whisk form, which is like fingers all coming out from a common hand.[24]

The structure of the literary world in Meiji Japan, which was dominated by *Ken'yūsha* – other groups lacked either such powerful contacts with the publishing industry, or strong leaders of Kōyō's calibre, or so many talented novelists – alienated writers who held different literary views and thus did not want to, and could not, become part of the literary establishment. Their opposition and criticism gradually paved the way to a change in the type of relations within the *bundan* and in its view of literature, a change which occurred only after Kōyō's death in 1903.

Mention should be made here of three people whose literary

careers and ideas proved to be very much against the tide of the time: Futabatei Shimei, Uchida Roan and Kitamura Tōkoku.

FUTABATEI SHIMEI (1864–1909)

Futabatei Shimei is the author of *Ukigumo*, which he wrote at the age of twenty-one, and which is considered to be the first realistic modern novel in Japan. It was the first novel to be written in the colloquial language (*kōgo*) and its major theme sanctioned an independent outlook among young Japanese of the new generation. In the figure of the hero one finds an idealisation of inner-directed conduct whereby one acts according to internalised principles of right and wrong rather than in conformity with the immediate social environment. The individual should rely on his own efforts, knowledge and skills rather than on the joint effort of the group. He should accept responsibility for his own actions rather than seek the security and guidance of the group.[25]

For Itō Sei, Futabatei's pioneering modernity is proved by the fact that he was 'the first writer really writing about the self and its conflicts with the world'. In his deep concern about the quality of human life, Futabatei 'went beyond the illusion of the *risshin shusse* [cult of advancement in life and social success] spirit', bringing forth the problems of the inner life of people in the Meiji period.[26]

Futabatei's career as a professional writer was very short: it started in 1885 when he left the Russian language and literature department at Gaigo Gakkō,[27] and under the guidance and protection of Tsubouchi Shōyō published the first volume of *Ukigumo*. It ended three years later when he accepted a government post.

Nakamura Mitsuo blames Futabatei's progressive ideas as being responsible for his tragic literary career: 'His point of view was far too advanced to be accepted generally at that time, and it was this unhappy circumstance that caused him to give up his literary activities later.'[28] They were also 'responsible for his isolated and unhappy position in the literary world of Japan, in which he always regarded himself as a literary outlaw'.

Futabatei's relations with the contemporary literary establishment were very uncomfortable. He disliked associating with most other writers and had few literary friends. Isolated and lonely, he consistently refused to be identified with members of literary circles.

His view of literature and the mission of the writer, permeated by nineteenth-century Russian idealism, was too advanced for the *Ken'yūsha*-dominated literary world. He was scornful of writers who considered only style and form and neglected the real purpose of literature, which lay in revealing the truth to the world. He also thought their way of living profoundly dishonest, corrupted by personal ambition or association with money. In his diary, published under the title *Ochiba no hakiyose* (A Pile of Fallen Leaves) in 1889, he wrote:

> There are only those useless books which people who play around write for food and money. . . . But the life of a literary man is to take up a pen and describe the characters and customs, the real situation of his nation, the way people live; to seek the truth where scholars and moralists cannot reach; to help those who have not enough self-confidence to go on living. Hence it is not true that writing a novel is a worthless occupation, but it is questionable whether a person like myself can become a real novelist.[29]

His lack of self-confidence came from his realisation of failure, as *Ukigumo* obviously did not meet the standards set by the masters of Russian literature like Turgenev, to whose work Futabatei was particularly attracted, or Dostoyevski. This, combined with the apparent success at the time of stories like Kōyō's *Iro zange*, which he despised, was the main cause of his despair and discouraged him from remaining a writer.

In addition Futabatei's income from writing had been very small despite the recognition which it brought him, and he suffered from the shame of being a burden to his family. As has been mentioned earlier, it was difficult to publish a full length novel if one was not employed by a newspaper or magazine, and Futabatei realised that he either had to throw himself more actively into writing for magazines and editing or he had to embark on some other career altogether.

The discrepancy between his principles, in which the Confucian concept of honesty by living according to one's convictions played an important part, and the way of living of the professional writers who were 'writing for profit' 'created internal conflicts that prevented him from working and were a major factor in his eventual decision to abandon all attempts to establish himself as a professional writer and take a position with the government'.[30].

Futabatei became a tragic figure, a symbol of the dilemma facing such a writer who had to choose between living according to his ideals and earning a living. Itō Sei summed up the situation when he described Futabatei as an honest and conscientious writer who 'was forced into silence because a modern *bundan* had not yet come into existence'.[31]

In the meantime, the contemporary literary establishment was criticised sharply by Futabatei's younger friend Uchida Roan. In the same year that Futabatei took up his government post, Uchida read Dostoyevski's *Crime and Punishment*, and three years later published a translation of the novel, which, as he said, changed his attitude to literature. It was undoubtedly owing to Futabatei's influence, whose doubts about how best to live and write afflicted not only himself but also his friends, that Uchida hated the way of life in the *bundan* and finally expressed it in a satirical pamphlet published in 1894 *Bungakusha to naru hō* (How to Become a Literary Man).

UCHIDA ROAN (1868–1929)

Uchida Roan, who by the time the pamphlet was published was a well-known literary critic and translator of Russian literature, kept his authorship of *Bungakusha to naru hō*, a book which shocked and offended many, a total secret, and for a long time his identity as the real author was not discovered.

The book is a satire on the lifestyle and professional conduct of the literary guild. In the preface the author refers to it as 'a textbook for literary adepts', and suggests that it is meant for those 'who are willing to spend their lives playing around, to forfeit their principles, and thus to become literary men'. The chapters deal with the various matters of which such young men should be aware before they embark on a literary career:

The art of learning what is happening in the world of literature;
The qualifications needed to become a literary man;
What a literary man should know when associating with others;
How to write and deal with publishers, etc.[32]

These seemingly serious chapter headings conceal in fact a highly satirical interpretation of the entire range of literary activities. They revealed the contradiction between the surface values of the *bundan* and what really existed underneath. Uchida's main attack is against the hypocrisy of the established literary figures who, while pretending not to be involved in the 'vulgar' realities of life, were in fact concerned with nothing but their popularity, to which they quickly became enslaved. He suggests that the main concern of the writer seemed to be whether his novel was to be printed, in how many copies, whether it was properly advertised and how it would sell. The one intention with which he put pen to paper was to become 'a master'. The word 'master' was used like a wig – every literary person wore it when on the stage, so the first thing a young adept approaching a literary man should do, was to cry out loud 'Master!'

To become a *bunshi* (a literary man, member of the *bundan*) it was necessary to display the qualities of insensitivity, carelessness and narrow-mindedness, and to transform oneself into a 'floating' type with no direction or principles like grass floating on the river. But to possess these qualities was not sufficient. To become a writer one had to know the ways of the literary world, one had to become a *tsū* (an expert or a connoisseur) in literary matters. There was an easy way to attain this object: one had to read certain articles of certain writers in certain papers and magazines, but one could also succeed without doing this, if one only looked carefully at advertisements and remembered the names which appeared there frequently. If one was not prepared to do that, one had to give up all thought of ever becoming a famous writer.

But most revealing is perhaps the chapter in which the young adept finds advice about how to associate with fellow writers. He should try, suggests Uchida, to form a small group, selecting the members not so much according to any shared ideas which they might have, but giving primary consideration to whether they all lived in the same *chō* (area) and whether they liked sake. Once the group has been formed, the activities of members should include theatre-going, flower viewing, tea drinking, publishing in the same paper, and, above all, praising each other's works. They may envy or even positively hate each other, but they should appear kind and sympathetic, and they should declare themselves to be such-and-such school in the *bundan*.

Those who wanted to join a school of the *bundan* should live near the *gohonzon*, the sacred centre of the group. They should go there and listen, sitting on their knees, bowing frequently, to lectures on literature or to sophisticated jokes. Finally they should supplicate with the words: 'Please, accept me', and the ceremony of joining was completed. An even simpler way was to apply for apprenticeship and thus from the start be accepted and supported. This was the quickest and therefore the best way.

The author also noticed that the company of literary men was very much limited to other literary men, and he expressed his admiration thus: 'Judging by common standards, it must be unbearable to stick to these micro-groups. But they (writers) are obviously able to endure it. They bear the unbearable and this is what makes them great.'

In 1894, when this sarcastic and ironical document appeared, the Meiji *bundan* had already acquired a degree of stability and inflexibility that had begun to be an obstacle to progress. *Bungakusha to naru hō* portrays in a masterly way the suffocating and oppressive atmosphere of the Meiji *bundan*.

KITAMURA TŌKOKU (1868–1894)

In the same year in which Uchida published his pamphlet (1894), Kitamura Tōkoku, a twenty-five-year-old poet, critic and thinker committed suicide. Itō Sei is confident that Kitamura's death is one more piece of evidence that a 'modern' literary world had not yet come into being:

> There were no conditions in Japanese society which would allow the existence of a man possessing ideas like his. So the reason why his precursor Futabatei Shimei became silent, and Kitamura killed himself may be explained as being because there was no sufficient escape place for them, a place for friends sharing a common life and consciousness, a place called the *bundan*.[33]

The outrageous ideas of Tōkoku, which Meiji society could not tolerate, were concentrated mainly round the concept of individual freedom and were deeply influenced by the Christian philosophy of Uchimura Kanzō, the main Christian thinker of the Meiji period. Uchimura placed the moral duties of the individual above other social values, saying 'God lives in the spirit of the individual before he dwells in the church'. He had the courage to maintain, against the ideas of the Meiji State, that individual conscience should be beyond any coercion: 'However good a principle, it cannot fail to become a bad principle if it is enforced from without.'

Uchimura rejected the moral authority of the State on the basis of his Christian faith. The famous 'Uchimura Incident' occurred when he refused to bow before the Emperor's portrait and the Imperial Rescript on Education on the occasion of the Emperor's birthday in November 1890. This brought upon Uchimura, then a teacher in the First Higher School in Tokyo, the charge of *lèse-majesté* and summary dismissal from his position. Japan in the 1890s provided an unlikely home for advocates of individual conscience and solitary opposition. The great period of Westernisation seemed to be over, the formation of the Meiji State was completed with the Constitution, the educational system, the powerful military establishment and the newly-formulated ideology of Imperial divinity and national uniqueness.

The nation was united under the authority of the Emperor, who was an embodiment of absolute values: 'The eternal culmination of the True, the Good, and Beautiful throughout all ages and in all places.'[34] National sovereignty was the ultimate source of both ethics and power. Morality was not summoned up from the depths of the individual; on the contrary, it had roots outside the individual. An open declaration of the fact that the Japanese State, being a moral entity, monopolised the right to determine values was provided by the Imperial Rescript on Education proclaimed before the summoning of the first Imperial Diet in 1890. Preaching 'the harmony and unity of loyalty and filial piety' it utilised the morality of the family and transformed it into the morality of the nation, thus laying the foundations of what was later defined as the 'family State'.

To suppress individual desires for the good of the family, to obey parents, to succeed in life for the sake of the family and thus repay parents' affection – these were the foundation of Japanese morality, imposed on the individual from outside. With the emergence of the new Meiji State, traditional values were not only not destroyed, but were in fact reinforced and utilised by the State. On the national level of the 'family State' they were transformed into loyalty to the throne.

Japanese scholars, looking at the Meiji period through the experience of recent history, speak of the distortion of modernisation in Japan. Faced with the immensely superior power of the Western world, Japan concentrated her efforts on becoming a 'militarily strong nation with a thriving economy' (*fukoku kyōhei*). To the most prominent Meiji enlightenment thinkers, including Fukuzawa Yukichi, modernisation meant the advancement of capitalism within which, they assumed, modern individualism would naturally develop.

However, as the sociologist Fukutake Tadashi has pointed out, that idealised picture of '*homo economicus*' failed to create substantial freedom and equality in Japan, where human welfare and social progress were sacrificed for the sake of economic development. The Japanese capitalist system failed to create individuals in the Western sense. The community foundation of society along with the family system, status consciousness and conformist conduct was preserved, and as a result no respect for human rights developed.[35]

The only political movement for freedom and democracy which existed was the popular rights movement for which Uchimura was a stalwart fighter and by which Tōkoku was strongly influenced during his school days. Its main emphasis, however, was on establishing democratic institutions of the Western type and it noticeably failed to produce any consistent ideological support for the rights of the individual versus the State. The power of the State was growing rapidly and the movement was soon suppressed.

By the time of the Sino-Japanese War (1894–5) many young Japanese had lost much of their predecessors' optimism about the possibility of reforming society. They felt powerless before the political and social order and oppressed by the growing power of the bureaucracy. Discovering few opportunities for self-expression in national affairs they found themselves increasingly alienated. Thus the 1890s may be considered as a transition period in the intellectual history of Japan during which the liberal type of intellectual with his strong sense of public vocation was replaced by the intellectual who was alienated and disillusioned. The career of Kitamura Tōkoku well illustrates this transition.

Like another writer of his generation, Kunikida Doppo, Kitamura abandoned his plans for a political career and sought refuge in writing. Literature was to be the vehicle for transmitting his ideas; he saw himself as the Victor Hugo of Japan. Later, under the influence of Christianity, literature became to him a medium for expressing individual conscience which he came to consider as the ultimate moral value.

Out of this consciousness that the liberal intellectual had failed grew Tōkoku's theory of a free individual – free from the tyranny of the State and society. In his essay 'Naibu seimei ron' (About the

Inner Life) he declares spiritual freedom to be the highest value in man's life. The role of the writer is that of a fighter for spiritual freedom (*seishin no senshi*); literature was to be a bastion of the spirit, where worldly success or achievement did not carry much significance.

Tōkoku established in literature the romantic ideal of a free and pure, lonely and heroic, individual; and by setting literature against society, he established a new basis for its existence. He led literature to a position of subjectivism and purity where it could not be measured by its utilitarian value, a position which was later taken up by the naturalist *bundan* writers.

This effort to establish the authority of literature was made by both Tōkoku and Futabatei, but whereas Futabatei aimed at a critical and realistic description of relations between the individual and society, Tōkoku glorified the lonely struggle of the individual against a society which prevented him living according to his ideals.

CONCLUSION

The first half of the Meiji period witnessed the formation of the first professional society of writers, whose members proposed to increase the social significance of literature and establish it as a legitimate branch of art capable of entertaining adults through works which were stylistically perfect. Their ideas, however, were confined within the old, traditional morality of Meiji society, and no attention was paid to the circumstances of the individual. In Itō Sei's view their art was a sincere attempt at conciliation between the artist and society, and this found expression also in the fact that their works were written in the *bungo* literary style. Affectation, etiquette and self-restraint, all hallmarks of this style, caused writers to think in terms of the feudal morality to which the style belonged and to create portraits of people who accepted traditional social norms. This type of literature existed until the mid-Meiji era.[36]

During this period the task of introducing modern ideas and promoting the cause of the individual was taken up by isolated writers, who drew their inspiration from their knowledge of European literature. They could not, however, develop their talents, trapped as they were between the semi-feudal literary establishment and the absence of a favourable social and political climate.

2 The Naturalist *Avant-garde* and the Formation of the Modern *Bundan*

INTRODUCTION

The death of Kitamura Tōkoku marked an end to the period which for the purposes of this volume has been referred to as Meiji Japan, the hopeful period when 'intellectuals in general had a high sense of national purpose, of obligation, of responsibility, and when there was a keenness, an enthusiasm, a zest for the adventure of modernisation, which made the intellectual a firmly wedded member of the leadership stratum'.[1] Tōkoku's death symbolised the failure of the intellectual to participate in and influence the course of his nation's history in the spirit of Western democratic liberalism.

Japan's victory in the Sino-Japanese War of 1894–5 marked the opening of the new Imperial period of her history, which ended only with her defeat in the Second World War and which brought a significant change in the intellectuals' attitude to their country. The decade between the Sino- and Russo-Japanese wars is usually considered critical for the formation of attitudes in Imperial Japan. First, with the constant growth in the numbers of those who had received higher education, the individual intellectual no longer had as much prestige as when he was a member of a much smaller class; now less of an élite, intellectuals were no longer as sure of employment as they had been and they also grew more critical of their society. Secondly, the change in the class composition of the intelligentsia, brought about by the new educational system, had important consequences. Whereas the earlier intellectuals had all been of relatively high class origin, now an increasing number began to come from non-*samurai* orders – merchants, the growing middle class, and land-owning families in the countryside.[2] The formerly close relations between intellectuals and politicians gave way to a polarisation, with politicians, bureaucrats and the growing military at one end, and at the other, the intellectuals, progressively withdrawing from public life into the new academies, into the professions, and, for public expression, into the world of journalism. An increasing number of intellectuals found themselves outside of and even hostile to political activity.[3]

In other words, the period between the Sino-Japanese and the Russo-Japanese Wars was characterised by a definite split between the protagonists of '*kokken*' and those of '*minken*', between the nationalists and the liberal intellectuals.[4] The former were supporters of the government and received a large measure of support from the masses. They concerned themselves mainly with what they considered to be national interests (*kokken*) which were to be advanced even at the expense of civil rights. The liberal intellectuals maintained a stance of defending civil rights (*minken*), but faced with the urgent necessity for the Japanese State to be strong, they were put under considerable strain and pressure. In this situation many of the intellectuals of the time gave tacit recognition to the authority of the State, but at the same time tried to disassociate themselves from it.

The phenomenon of the separation of the State and the intellectuals was clearly manifested by the emergence of what Maruyama Masao in his essay 'Patterns of Individuation' ('individuation' understood as emancipation of the individual in the process of modernisation) defined as a 'privatised individual'. In Maruyama's definition a privatised type is oriented towards the achievement of self-gratification rather than public goals; his scope of interest is rather confined to his private affairs; he is characterised by political apathy, which is a conscious reaction against the increasing bureaucratisation of the system and against the complexities of the social and political process in which he finds himself involved.[5]

In the world of letters, privatisation corresponds to what conventional Japanese histories of literature describe as the 'emergence of individualism' or the 'rise of self-consciousness', which were represented by a wide range of literary works, from the romantic self-expression of the Myōjō group of poets to the disillusioned and disgusted self of the Japanese naturalists. The naturalist novel which came to dominate after the Russo-Japanese War represents most clearly the trend of privatisation.[6]

Among many factors which promoted the tendency towards privatisation, the most conspicuous was perhaps the generation problem. For those who arrived at manhood in the 1900s, the early struggle for modernisation, for national independence, which the previous generation had experienced, all belonged to the past. After the turn of the century young people, in numbers significant enough to attract attention, lost interest in national issues and retreated into the private concern of their own lives.[7]

The retreat from social matters, which became conspicuous at the time when the State itself was glorying in its victory over Russia (1905), is evidence of a radical change in intellectual attitudes. It represented the phenomenon of intellectual alienation, with which modern societies of the West are also familiar. Raymond Williams, writing about Europe, describes it as a situation in which the economic or liberal individualism of the early stage of modernisation gives way to modern individualism with its emphasis on a negative freedom, on the right of the individual to be left alone and to retreat from social thinking. The image of society is then of something inherently bad: a restrictive, interfering, indifferent entity. It is also commonly assumed that things will remain much as they are, that fundamental change is inconceivable, but that individuals, if they turn back on themselves and on 'real' interests, can get by or even be happy.[8]

Malcolm Bradbury finds that the sense of internal difficulty experienced by intellectuals in conceiving their own role (on the one hand they have an increasing sense of marginality and isolation, on the other they feel responsible for the emergence of new modes of thought and the elimination of false ones) manifests itself in Europe and America in the idea of *avant-garde* or bohemian communities. These provide artists with a liberating environment for the independent pursuit of their art. This marks the point where the artist wins total freedom to be an artist unconditionally, but it also marks the loss of a social overview on his part. Socially it means the growth of specialised communities of arts, where independent mores and life-styles can be lived out and where art is both produced and consumed largely by other artists.[9]

The change that occurred in the role and status of the artist in Western societies and resulted in the formation of bohemian communities corresponds in general terms to the situation that developed in Japan after the Russo-Japanese war. Arima Tatsuo in his book on modern Japanese literature speaks of 'a total flight from society' on religious, aesthetic or ideological grounds, as the only alternative left to a Japanese intellectual who wanted to make a break with convention. But it meant, he points out, turning away from existing social reality and striving for an emancipation that never came to grips with the realities of the socialised self.[10]

The naturalist movement that emerged in the wake of the Russo-Japanese war had all the features of a bohemian mentality. The economic boom that followed victory created favourable conditions for the growth of the publishing industry, thus creating new opportunities for writers. They now discovered that they could earn their living just by writing novels without having to seek employment in journalism. Now independent of the demands of their newspapers and the necessity to appeal to the tastes of the newspaper-reading public, they were able to carry out their artistic experiments with a considerable amount of freedom. The writers of the new naturalist movement, such as Shimazaki Tōson, Tayama Katai, Tokuda Shūsei, Masamune Hakuchō and others, did not have any regular paid employment; their social ties became confined to their immediate families, and the circle of their literary friends.[11]

The other factor that propelled the 'naturalistic revolution' was the death of Ozaki Kōyō in 1903. Without his leadership the *Ken'yūsha* group disintegrated, and in so doing relinquished the hold which it had over the literary world and freed writers from the restricting formal ties of *oyabun–kobun* relations. Some, such as Tokuda Shūsei and Tayama Katai, joined the new naturalistic movement; others retired into the world of popular fiction.

The naturalists inherited from Kitamura Tōkoku his pessimistic view of society and his belief in literature as the only possible means of emancipation of the individual. It may be interesting to note that they themselves had never experienced Kitamura's kind of dramatic failure and disillusionment in actual life. In the early stages of their lives, in the hopeful years of Meiji, they often expressed interest in following politically and socially active careers. But as far as the ruling élite was concerned, these intellectuals were outsiders from the beginning: their family background was as a rule that of second sons of former *samurai*; their childhood experience was of the gloomy life of declining families which did not prosper after the Restoration and did not quite understand the changes taking place around them; none of them went to a national university – they were students at missionary and private universities, which at that time were still strongholds of liberal thought and opposition to the government.

They compensated for this feeling of alienation by discarding the reality of Japanese society as backward and feudal and opening their minds and hearts to the Western-inspired mission of the liberation of the individual from the oppressive social system. They saw themselves as rebels in the cause of emancipation and progress. They drew their spiritual inspiration from the nineteenth-century European realistic novel and hoped to follow the path of writers like Flaubert, Balzac, Maupassant and Zola. In their view the fundamental goal of modern literature was to express the truth about human nature and social reality. Rebellious in spirit, they intended to smash all obstacles to the attainment of this goal.

Tayama Katai in his memoirs reflects:

Why was our group formed? We were not related in any way, we did not have the same school career nor the same kind of personal history – how then did our group come to exist?

We were like a river created by streams flowing from various directions, having no common source, at one time flowing independently and then joining into a big river. Kunikida came from *Kokuminha*,[12] Shimazaki from *Bungakukai*,[13] and I, if anything, from *Ken'yūsha*, but we all mixed together. What brought us together was the search for what was 'new' and 'honest'; the same view of foreign literature; and also hatred of the numerous cliques of the *bundan* and a desire to separate from them. We got on naturally and peacefully. First Kunikida published *Unmei*, then Shimazaki *Hakai*, and then I *Futon*.[14]

The respective dates of the publications were: *Unmei* (Fate) 1906, *Hakai* (Apostasy) 1906 and *Futon* (The Quilt) 1907. Hence 1906 is usually accepted as the first year of Japanese naturalism. Apart from Kunikida Doppo, Shimazaki Tōson and Tayama Katai, other naturalistic writers such as Iwano Hōmei, Tokuda Shūsei and Masamune Hakuchō started their literary careers as naturalists at the same time.

The naturalist postulate of reality and truth-searching was far removed from the *Ken'yūsha* standards of elegant and entertaining popular literature. In Itō Sei's words, the main difference between the naturalist rebels and outcasts and the writers of the established literary world, lay in the fact that within the same institution of the professional literary market, the former began to realise and express their own individual selves. They formed a special group where for the first time literature exploring the individual and concerned with the writer's ego could come into existence.[15] The naturalists revolutionised Japanese ideas about character in the novel and the general role of literature, and their influence diminished only after the arrival of the Marxist writers in the 1920s, when the second literary 'revolution' took place.

Of the three novels mentioned in the above quotation, Shimazaki Tōson's *Hakai* was nearest to the Western concept of a modern realistic novel. The protagonist of this novel, recently translated into English, is a young, sensitive outcast (*eta*) who tries to hide his social origin at the command of his father in order to win social acceptance and success. In the end, however, he breaks the commandment as this is the only way in which he will be able to live more honestly and regain his dignity. Woven into a wide social panorama of Meiji Japan, this fictionalised narrative of individual struggle for freedom and independence against the moral precepts of feudal society was a far cry from the sentimental novels of Ozaki Kōyō, which never questioned the social order.

By comparison with *Hakai*, Tayama Katai's *Futon* is conspicuous for its lack of social overview. There the narrator speaks directly to the reader, in the first person, about his hopeless plight as a family man and a teacher involved in an affair with one of his girl students. By confessing this shameful fact, the author exposed to the public eye his own weakness and egoism. At the risk of offending the moral code of his day, destroying his position as the head of the family and ruining the harmony of his family life, the author put into practice his ideas about literature having to reveal the true nature of man.

Tayama Katai's *Futon* had the greatest impact on the further development of modern Japanese literature. It served as an orthodox pattern for the type of literature which acquired the symbolic name *watakushi shōsetsu* (the I-novel).

The I-novel was a peculiar product of Japanese naturalism, in which the environment was described through the author's personal experience. It was usually narrated in the first or third person singular and informed the reader about certain events of the author's life. In their search for reality and truth the naturalists came to the conclusion that to describe truly is to describe only what one thought, felt and did oneself. Truth could not be grasped through a description of others, and as truth was the essence of pure literature, anything that went beyond the description of personal experience was fabrication and falsehood and belonged to the inferior, popular literature (*tsūzoku shōsetsu*). The novelist and critic Kume Masao expressed this rebellious spirit of the *bundan* when he said that Tolstoy's *War and Peace* was nothing but a very well written popular novel. Subjective I-novel confession became the standard form of expression of Japanese naturalists. Its character differs greatly from the autobiographical novel as it is known in Europe.

Maruyama Masao points out that the ideas behind the confession were quite different from individualism in the European sense of the term. The expression favoured by Japanese naturalists – 'the sorrow and disillusionment of exposing realities' (*genjitsu bakuro no hiai*) – well describes the hero of such a novel, who is neither a masculine individualist, facing the challenges of life with grand dreams for the future, nor the Nietzschean superman, courageously trampling over conventional moral restraints. Tayama Katai describes the hero, modelled after himself, in a tone of disgust and self-aversion; disillusioned by the social climate, he confines himself to his own small room, delving into the rotten carnality of his own desire.[16]

Thus from the outset Japanese naturalism acquired distinct features of its own, and as a result it did not resemble very much its European counterpart. The question which has preoccupied Japanese literary historians ever since is why modern Japanese literature never developed the potential of *Hakai* to become, like its Western counterpart, a force for social criticism, but instead withdrew into the inward-looking, self-oriented, anti-social literary form of the I-novel. It has been suggested that the answer to this question lies partly in the existence of the *bundan* and partly in the nature of Japan's literary tradition.

The claims of the naturalists were fundamentally incompatible with the social and political ethos of Imperial Japan and this led to the writers' withdrawal from society into the *bundan*. The end result of this trend was the eventual split not only between politics and literature but also between society and literature. For the young naturalist writers in the first decade of this century the truth-searching postulate, rather than being accepted as a purely literary method, was welcomed as a new way of living. The problem of literary technique, of how to write, was superseded by a problem of a moral nature, of how to live the life of a modern man in a modern age. In a fashion similar to that of nineteenth-century Russia where the problems posed by the encounter with Western ideas were treated by the writers as real-life issues, Japanese writers judged the sincerity of their works by the moral stand which they took in real life. One had to prove one's devotion to the new ideas by living them; a writer's work and his life became inseparable, judged by the same criterion of being true to his beliefs. In his study of the modern Japanese novel the contemporary novelist and critic Nakamura Mitsuo describes this new attitude as follows:

> For them the novel was not merely an artistic representation of human life. Rather it was a means of searching for a new, valid way of living. At the same time it was the record of this search. This was the hazardous quest for the sake of which the writers of the Meiji and Taishō periods risked tragedy in their real lives. They had high, probably exaggerated, expectations of the novel, and they dared to believe in them and to live them.[17]

This new morality, therefore, required that the writer live and write in a new way according to the dictates of his individual conscience. The practical unity of life and thought, however, which it demanded, could not be accommodated within the framework of the Japanese social structure. The mechanisms of social control both external (the political and legal systems under which one is obliged to live) and internal (morality, customs, manners) were much more oppressive than in a liberal society and acted against the self-establishment of the individual.

The new morality could only be practised by writers inside a small, experimental environment, where it was possible, although frequently at considerable psychological cost, to ignore almost completely the day-to-day expectations of society. Japanese literary scholars seek the main reason for the formation of the modern *bundan* – a self-enclosed community of professional writers, where the writers could live according to their own ethical standards – in the need for such an environment. To quote from Nakamura Mitsuo again:

> A special society of their own, the *bundan* or literary world, was necessary in order to make possible this idealistic life attitude, that is to make it possible for the writer to keep his head always full of the very latest ideas abroad in the world at large, while

living himself in the society of an island kingdom in the Far East –
and in a very secluded corner of that society, indeed.[18]

The image of Japanese writers as inhabiting a 'secluded corner' of
society refers perhaps to the generally unenviable status that the
literary profession enjoyed in Imperial Japan:

> Quarrelling with my parents and rebelling against my
> preceptors, I chose of my own free will the state of a poet, a
> vocation which the state never required of me – a vocation which
> it rather sought to suppress violently . . . 'traitors worse than
> gamblers', 'treacherous vagrants' – these are the titles of honour
> which we shall have to stomach forever.[19]

These words of the novelist Nagai Kafū express vividly the
position of writers in a society where the act of choosing a literary
career was considered to be a sign of social maladjustment, failure or
rebellion. Far from receiving governmental encouragement, literature was more often an object of suppression. It grew up as
'something exclusively unofficial, sometimes even in the role of a
sort of outcast kept deliberately in obscurity'.

In contrast with Europe, the majority of writers in Japan did not
develop a strong social conscience. They began their professional
lives as exiles from society. European exiles like Byron, Wilde and
Maupassant abandoned their countries and from their exile were
active as severe critics of their societies. In Japan after the
establishment of naturalism the majority of novelists lived as
internal exiles. They abandoned the universities, regular employment or family businesses and led a dissolute life that ruined their
health. In their writings, however, they did not criticise society.
They fled from it and entered a small community, the *bundan*, that
had the special atmosphere of a haven for social recluses. This new
bundan came into being about 1907.[20]

BUNDAN

The naturalist movement did not last long. It was soon succeeded
by various anti-naturalist schools which opposed its narrow outlook
and lack of social overview, but it did succeed in changing radically
the character of the novel and of the literary world. To it we owe the

formation of a literary bohemian community of special mores and behaviour, which became particularly prominent in the Taishō period.

This new *bundan* had certain features in common with the Meiji *bundan* in the 1880s and 1890s, which was described in the previous chapter. It was still the element of social and economic insecurity which impelled the writers to form professional communities of their own to defend their interests and to gain recognition. But what united the young writers in the Meiji forties and at the same time made their *bundan* so different from the *Ken'yūsha's* world was their search for a new way of living, their sense of a new mission to create a new literature which would speak the truth about society and themselves and which would liberate them from the yoke of feudal morality.

They created for themselves an environment where they were able to pursue their aims in an atmosphere of mutual understanding, in a manner comparatively independent from events in the outer world.

Itō Sei saw the importance of the *bundan* in terms of its break with society. He defined it as a community of idealists who had severed their social ties in order to live and create freely:

It was a small group of writers and consisted only of people with a special life-style and consciousness which was unacceptable to real society in Japan. Their readers were very few and themselves all aspirants of the same special life. They were a group of young people who held the illusion that they would become free human beings while . . . actually living as exiles from the real world. . . . As a rule these writers were social failures unconcerned with social morality, inhabitants of an outcast community. . . . Their ideology of self-determination of the individual did not belong to the whole society. It was a possession of their particular guild which existed in a nook of society. . . . In this way the writers, by separating themselves from the prevailing mentality of the period, for the first time actually achieved the consciousness of modern man.[21]

The separation from society brought two major results. First, it removed the writers from the social scene as a force of any direct influence or importance, as they had renounced their interest in the affairs of the nation. Secondly, the writers lost, socially, the power of appealing to a great number of people and came to focus on the denizens of their own world. The content of their works became limited by the framework of the community or guild which they inhabited. In the search for truth and reality they were thrown back upon the literary analysis of the self, the ultimate product of which was the I-novel.

The split between the writers and society was accompanied by a split between literature and politics. This became particularly conspicuous at the time of the Great Treason Incident in 1910, when a group of anarchic socialists led by Kōtoku Shūsui was accused of a plot against the Emperor's life and after months of secret trials executed. The almost complete silence with which the literary world accepted the incident was a matter of much self-recrimination to a writer like Nagai Kafū who some years later mentioned it in *Hanabi* (The Fireworks):

> As a man of letters, I ought not to have remained silent. But I kept silent as other literary men did. I felt I was not able to bear the pain of my conscience. I felt extremely ashamed of being a man of literature.[22]

This is a remark that has been made much of in explaining Kafū's later withdrawal from the literary world. But the reaction of Kafū, who still at heart had Zola's model '*J'accuse*' with which to compare himself, was quite different from, for instance, that of his younger colleague Tanizaki Jun'ichirō, a prominent Taishō and Shōwa novelist, who referred to the Kōtoku affair as a mere outside event unrelated to his manner of life as an artist.

The lack of interest in the State together with the absence of State patronage led to a complete separation between the State and literature. In contrast with the previous generation, politics came to be viewed by the writers as something dirty and untrustworthy in which they refused to participate. And it was not until the *bundan* was challenged by the Marxist literary movement that the problem of literature and politics was ever considered again.

The naturalists were courageous – it demanded courage to inquire with harsh honesty into carnal desire and to impugn as unreasonable and inhuman the accepted social norms, but it was a kind of courage that never disturbed the social order:

> The fact that these elements which were potentially most dangerous for the society, formed a small group which had no

contact with the environment, which lived only for itself and which published works that no one really understood using a coded language comprehensible only to itself, meant that they were harmless as far as society itself was concerned.

They did publish chronicles of their immoral and reckless lives, but those works did not reach society. They lived without criticising politics, without intending to improve the society, indulging only in their inferiority complex.[23]

The naturalists' literature did not ever imply revolt against the authority of the Meiji system because of its private orientation and its indulgence in masochistic self-disclosure, which created an image of man defeated by his desires and the environment.

A young contemporary radical poet, Ishikawa Takuboku (1886–1912), interpreted naturalist literature as a reflection of the feelings found in 'most of the comparatively cultured youths', the feelings that 'the nation must be strong and great. We have not a single reason to hinder the growth of Japan. But we would rather be excused from lending aid to it.' He perceived that behind their declaration that 'we have nothing to do with powerful authority' there lay a kind of passive conformism.[24]

The writers avoided a confrontation with the State by retreating deep into their own world and judging their behaviour only according to the rules of this world. In Itō Sei's view this instinct of self-preservation saved modern Japanese literature:

> The pure life of the *bundan* was certainly unusual. But had it been connected with society, it would have been destroyed. The activities of Kōtoku Shūsui furnish an example here. This separation made contemporary Japanese literature possible.[25]

THE I-NOVEL AS AN ORGANIC *BUNDAN* FORM

In spite of its professed admiration for European literary patterns, the special nature of the *bundan* produced a genuinely Japanese form of modern literature, the I-novel. Hirano Ken calls *Giwaku* (Doubt, 1913) by Chikamatsu Shukō the first fully-crystallised I-novel which developed from the naturalistic prototype of Tayama Katai. The novel represented the naturalistic view of the sinful nature of man, but it went further than Katai's confession, in exposing the dark, shameful side of human nature. It describes in a deeply moving fashion the author's search for his estranged wife. Torn between love and doubt he searches the inns of the area where he has heard she may be staying with her student lover. What makes *Giwaku* into a model I-novel is not only its style as an auto-biographical confession, but the depth of the self-exposure, which does not seem to be inhibited by shame or fear of what others may think. It is relentless in the revelation of the ugliness and weakness of men, and it leaves the reader perplexed at the tenacity of this almost pointless shamelessness. Nobody before Chikamatsu, says Hirano Ken, had ever attempted to hold the bare sword of human consciousness over the writer himself in such a fashion. His aimless destructive pursuit could only take place among those who had abandoned society and forgone all social ambitions – that is, within the *bundan*.[26]

In Hirano Ken's view Itō Sei's merit lies in perceiving the rise of the I-novel as a phenomenon closely connected with the rise of the *bundan*. For those who belonged to the *bundan* life was a kind of endless experiment in a true way of living, concerning which they presented evidence in the novels which they wrote about themselves:

> Those who entered that world . . . displayed its qualities to the full, in their self-destruction, in slandering friends, in coveting fame, in malicious gossip, in spreading doubts and rumours, committing suicide, abandoning their children, running away, being left by their wives, or dying of distress and poverty. And then under the name of novel, but almost completely deprived of any fictional form, they were recording these things as confessions, reports on their lives, and diaries. . . . It was each other's lives not works, that they recognised, and they estimated their companions according to the substance of their lives. Merciless mutual criticism, as harsh as that of life in a religious order, took place through these factual, autobiographical works. Within the *bundan* even the most ugly confession was possible; and there was also the possibility that one would be correctly criticised. What can be the reason for them having lived such pure lives in the *bundan*?[27]

The specific life conditions in the *bundan*, the lack of concern with the outside world, the very small number of readers – all these factors made the writer abandon the principle of fictional narrative and concentrate on his inner crises, thus fulfilling the main condition set for modern literature.

In spite of the special vocabulary (like a dialect) of these 'life reports', in spite of their abandonment of fictional technique in order to deprive outsiders of the possibility of understanding and in spite of the extreme limitation in the choice of subject – or no, rather because of the strength of concentration that resulted from the economical use of their powers, they were not behind world literature at the time.

How can it be appreciated by foreigners if it was not appreciated by the Japanese themselves? It is closed to the world. But if one somehow supplied the key, for example by means of information about the *bundan* in detailed notes and commentaries, then it would become clear that it represented a section of 20th century world literature, albeit an odd one.[28]

It is clear from the above quotation that in Itō Sei's view the importance of a knowledge of the *bundan* for the potential reader of modern Japanese literature cannot be over-emphasised. The novels generated there were written on the assumption that the reader possessed that knowledge:

It [the I-novel] was written on the assumption that, without explanation concerning the hero's environment or position, the reader knew the hero's personal history. So the hero . . . is almost not described in the novel. To read, one had to possess knowledge about the style of life of the dealers in literature – the Japanese novelist – who lived inside a special guild which they had organised. One had to know the gossip about the author current in literary circles, or to know the hero from the author's previous works.[29]

To achieve a sense of literary reality, the I-novel had to convince the reader that the events described in the novel were based on the direct experience of the author himself. That is why the 'I' of the I-novel is always a writer – the author himself – and why the acts the 'I' performs are real events in the reader's mind.

The I-novel developed from an instinctive expectation in the reader, who either, like the writer, had turned away from the society or who was young and eager to belong to the *bundan* himself. To a writer 'readers' meant not only those who understood his art and bought his books, but his comrades and sympathisers who had a similar view of life. Writers and readers were united in their contempt for 'vulgar persons', the worldly men of power, and in their trust in art.[30]

Bundan literature was not intended to become national literature. It concentrated on the particular consciousness of the people who belonged to it; it expressed the reality of their own lives and this was revealed in the I-novel style. To fabricate fiction, to create plots which would be of interest for a wider public would for them be a sign of corruption and compromise with society; to hide behind the mask of a fictional hero the sign of spiritual cowardliness.

The number of their readers remained small (about 1000 copies was the highest number of a first printing even in the period of the great popularity of the I-novel in the 1930s) in spite of the fast-growing newspaper-reading public. Their novels, says Itō Sei, were kept away from the readers not because of their immorality, but because of their dullness and monotony. For newspaper readers a separate group of writers of entertaining literature came into being. The division between the pure *bundan* literature and popular literature became thus firmly established in modern Japanese literature, creating two worlds which were incompatible and which mutually ignored each other. There was a kind of silent agreement between the *bundan* and society, based on this mutual lack of interest, which preserved the pure life of the *bundan* writers. The only exceptions to this were when, as occasionally happened, a particularly sensational *bundan* event or piece of gossip, like Tōson's intimate relations with his niece or Arishima's love suicide, aroused curiosity in society, and the books were bought to learn something more about this unknown world. Sometimes, also, the work of a *bundan* writer, who was not able to bear the discipline needed to write a pure novel, appeared in the newspapers and thus naturally became known to the newspaper readers. But when in contact with society in this way such a writer would keep silent about life and thought in the *bundan*.[31]

CONCLUSION

At the end of the Meiji era a dramatic change occurred in the world of literature. A group of young and talented new writers such as Shimazaki Tōson, Kunikida Doppo and Tayama Katai appeared, who had been nourished on European concepts of realism and individualism. While Kōyō-type literature degenerated into the popular novel (*tsūzoku shōsetsu*), the young writers raised the flag of 'pure' literature, which would provide an independent imperative from which society and life could be judged.

The *kōgo* style, which after being introduced into literature in the 1880s by Futabatei Shimei and Yamada Bimyō became rather unpopular in the succeeding period of growing national interests, now blossomed again in the works of the naturalists, as the best means of approaching and expressing reality.

Writers were increasingly drawn to the fast-developing city of Tokyo, which was the centre of cultural life. The urban environment enabled the writer to achieve his own emancipation and his expatriation from the province; it provided the possibility of living by writing; it drew artists together, and tended to produce artistic communities.

The end of the Meiji period witnessed the emergence of a new type of urban artistic community, which developed fully in the Taishō era – that of an intellectual proletariat, living on minimal resources, using its freedom to create an independent style of life and art. This was a phenomenon similar in a way to the bohemian communities of Europe and America. To this community, the *bundan*, can be ascribed the creation of the first, fully modern, literary genre in Japan, the I-novel.

In discussing the development of the *bundan*, one peculiarity of the Japanese situation should be noted. Modern Japanese writers never had an opportunity to apply their liberal, individualistic ideas to their society. From the start they were forced to create a community of their own in which to put their thought into practice. A social environment which did not value the novelist's profession, combined with the strong pressures of modernisation which regarded utilitarian values as being of the utmost importance, left no place for the small, idealistic community of writers with their spiritual dilemmas. Therefore, in modern Japan the nineteenth-century European type of the liberal intellectual who served as the moral conscience of his society never fully developed. The writers paid for their precarious independence by being branded as social outcasts. The psychological cost of such separation cannot be doubted. A special *bundan* mentality maintained and nurtured for years in the isolation of the *bundan* was the result.

The next chapters will deal with the *bundan*'s philosophy of life and art, and its internal development.

3 From Flight to Self-destruction

Thus, the theory of the *bundan* evolved in the first post-war years in the writings of men like Itō Sei, Hirano Ken, Nakamura Mitsuo and others. The escapist character of life in the Japanese literary community forms the nucleus of this theory, which examines the roots of escapist behaviour and its link with traditional oriental patterns of thought. Equally it examines the *bundan*'s artistic ideology – the belief in the supreme value of art and the effect which it had on the artists themselves.

Itō Sei's contribution lies in distinguishing between two social postures represented within the *bundan*: abandonment (*hōki*), which was realised through self-destructive flight from society and faithfully recorded in the naturalistic I-novel, and harmony (*chōwa*), which found its expression in the so-called *shinkyō shōsetsu*. The latter was a particular type of I-novel, which reflected on the author's state of mind and feelings and was written in retrospect, usually long after the events described in it took place.[1] In the course of its development, the *bundan* revealed a strong predisposition towards the posture of abandonment and flight, exhibiting a type of mentality which Itō Sei defined as the mentality of the 'fugitive slave' (*tōbō dorei*). The escapist mentality found its best means of expression in the literary genre of the I-novel:

Hōki (abandonment) ——>*tōbō dorei ishiki* (fugitive slave mentality) ——>I-novel.

TŌBŌ DOREI

The phrase '*tōbō dorei*' has attracted much attention in post-war Japanese literary studies. It seems that in coining this phrase Itō Sei had several factors in mind, prominent among which was the low social origin of the writers concerned, which in a sense facilitated their subsequent flight.

The naturalist writers who formed the *bundan* belonged to the provincial middle and lower classes – for instance, Iwano Hōmei's father was a minor police official, Tayama Katai was the second son of a low ranking *samurai*, Chikamatsu Shūkō's and Kamura Isota's families had been farmers for generations, Kasai Zenzō's father was a small-town businessman and merchant. These were the classes which, even after the Meiji Restoration, preserved many elements of feudal morality, leaving little scope for the romantic self-expression of young individualists. Only by defying their family duties and opting out of the inherited social structure altogether, could such writers hope to attain the freedom which they desired.

By the sheer totality of their defiance they condemned the reality of life in modern Japan, where a man planning a successful career had to follow a strictly-limited path – through the mill of unrewarding courses and difficult examinations at High School, followed by an even more difficult entrance examination to the University, only to be faced after graduation with yet another examination which would open the gates to soul-destroying employment in an office or company. Failing that, they could take over parental firms where they would become enmeshed in the traditional network of local relationships with its emphasis on duty, obligation and submission. To these intellectuals, educated on European ideas, this way of life seemed senseless, humiliating and inhuman. Had they followed the established patterns they would have become like slaves deprived of their freedom. Itō Sei wrote of them: 'Therefore I think of these writers as slaves who escaped from Japanese society, fugitive slaves.'[2]

A line of writers from Chikamatsu Shūkō (1876–1944) through Kasai Zenzō (1887–1928) and Kamura Isota (1897–1933) to Dazai Osamu (1909–1948) represents the escapist tradition in modern Japanese literature. In the lives and works of these authors one can discern certain common patterns which constitute the basic characteristic features of *tōbō dorei* behaviour and mentality.

First of all, as we have seen, they were usually of country origin and they escaped to Tokyo leaving their families behind. In Tokyo, however, they were able to find no real base for their lives either material or psychological. They subsisted on the poverty line (because they produced little and were, anyway, poorly rewarded for it), living and working in cheap lodging-houses and haunted by debts. Failing health (most of them fell victim to tuberculosis and died before they reached the age of forty), drink, drugs, unstable family life, affairs with women were the usual attributes of the life of the fugitive slave. They were social failures from the start and confronted with the harsh reality of the metropolis, they refused to overcome their difficulties rationally. Instead they turned their lives into 'positive failures', and the failure became food for their art.

Within the limits of their wretched existence they were able to live and create freely. Naturally from the social standpoint they found their lives far from desirable. They felt miserable for having transgressed the laws of socially-accepted behaviour; they suffered from a sense of guilt for having brought shame and unhappiness to their families. Yet in their minds they were proud of being artists and it was for their art's sake that they had to live as they did.

They approached their lives convinced that in order to create great art the happiness of home and family would have to be sacrificed. They saw their lives in terms of a sacrificial offering paid on the altar of art, and in one sense the depth of misery which they reached in their lives became the criterion by which they judged the sincerity of their convictions.

A typical example of the escapist's plight can be found in the life and works of Kasai Zenzō, a prominent I-novelist of the Taishō period. Yamamoto Kenkichi in his book *Shishōsetsu sakka ron* (On the I-novelists) describes Kasai Zenzō as a person who undoubtedly lived life in his own way but in a sense was incapable of living: heavy drinking, very small literary production, unstable family life and constant lack of money led him to illness and early death.[3]

In his best known work *Ko o tsurete* (Taking the Children, 1918) Kasai describes a stage in the life of a person closely resembling himself. The protagonist is in the depths of misery, although to outsiders he appears as leading an idle life. He is somehow unable to write his novel. His wife, who had returned to her family to raise a loan, eventually abandoned him. Left with the two children he is evicted by the landlord. With nowhere to go, he sells the remaining household goods, and with the resulting small amount of cash in his pocket leaves the house taking the children with him. The following passage ends the novel:

> He sold the wicker trunk and the wicker chest, the rice box and the rice cooker and all the other kitchen utensils of any value to

the owner of the local household store. Then, hoping to avoid a
crowd of creditors, he locked the house up and about eight o'clock
they left. He carried a basket containing the manuscript which he
had just started, pen and ink. His son, a second-year primary
school pupil dressed in *hakama* [formal Japanese dress], put the
satchel containing his school books and implements on his back.
He hurriedly tied up the hair of his seven year old daughter,
which had been neglected for days, and the three of them holding
hands walked towards the area which was bustling with night life
and thronged with people. He felt very tired. What was more, as
they had not yet eaten their evening meal, all three felt very
hungry.

They went into a bar, near the station. For the children he
ordered *sushi* [an expensive dish of portions of cold rice covered
with fish or egg] and for himself *sake*. He felt that in his present
mood nothing but *sake* could raise his spirits. He drank it greedily,
at the same time savouring each cup as though it was something
extremely precious. In a large mirror in front of him he saw a
reflection of his own face – pale and dark with hollow cheeks and
sunken eyes. He looked at it with a distant feeling as though it
belonged to someone else. He sat there pushing his hair away
from his face with his left hand and holding the *sake* cup in his
right hand. A sense of great tiredness came over him and he felt no
longer capable of thinking or fearing anything. He just kept
uttering deep meaningless sighs.

'Father, I feel like some fried prawns' – having finished the
sushi his son turned to him reading the menu.

'All right, all right. Fried prawns twice' – he called automatically to the waitress.

'Father, I feel like some beans' – his son asked again after a
while.

'All right. Beans twice and a bottle of *sake*' –he called out in the
same tone of voice.

It was not long before the children, their hunger satisfied, went
out and started playing tag. The girl would come up from time to
time and press her face against the glass door, to see what was
happening to her father. And having seen him still sitting there
and drinking she would return, smiling and reassured, to play
with her brother.

A dancer, vulgarly made up, came in announcing her arrival
by beating together a pair of wooden clappers. She was followed

by a girl of sixteen or seventeen playing a *shamisen* and singing. A drunken customer gave her money and she began dancing, moving her arms and swaying her hips. From time to time he could see her fox-like sharp face painted white for the occasion, and the strange squinting expression of her eyes as she danced in the narrow space between the door and the tables.

He emptied another bottle, having by now lost count of how many he had drunk. He just kept drinking from the little cup, from time to time turning his empty gaze towards the dancer.

'Nothing in this world interests or moves me any more' – he muttered to himself.

Some years previously, when he was still single, he used to go round these places drinking. He was not entirely more free or happy then than in his present life. Nevertheless words with which he used to express his feelings at the time, like grief or misery, sprang from a real interest which had the resilience of a rubber ball. Today, however, there was a hole in the rubber ball, which, when pressed, stayed dented; it had lost its original strength and vitality. Healthy interests and unhealthy interests – this may sound a little odd. But if a man cannot live by healthy interests he had to live and pursue the unhealthy ones. Life would become truly unbearable otherwise. However, the fact that man has to feed himself deprives him of healthy interests and equally of the resilience to pursue the unhealthy ones thus transforming him into a punctured rubber ball.

'Yes, the life of an artist who has lost interest is worse than the life of a peasant or a rickshaw man. It is worse than the worst life imaginable. It is a truly terrible life' – he muttered to himself as he watched the dancers, on whose ugly dance he had fixed his vacant gaze, leave the room.

'My own children might end up like this dancer.' As he painted this sad picture in his mind, he could not help hating his wife who had returned to her country home with his younger daughter and from whom he had not heard since. At the same time he reflected:

'It was all a result of my own worthlessness. She was only a woman. And in the same way as I was not prepared to kill my own self for the sake of my wife and children, she could not starve to death because of her husband and children.'

'Father, let's go now.'

'Are you getting tired?'

'Yes.'

Nagged by the children he finally forced himself to get up and rather drunk left the bar. They got on the train.

'Where are we going, father?'

'To a lodging house I know.'

'Lodging house? Oh. . . . '

The children asked repeatedly and anxiously on the train.

The three of them left the train at Shibuya station and walked up the slope, covered as usual with gravel, to K's lodgings. The owner of the house and his wife were acquaintances of his.

He went up to the desk and explained:

'My wife had to return to her home in the country as somebody fell ill there. Could you have us for two or three days?'

But the owner having at once appraised their situation as being far from normal, flatly refused saying that he had no vacancies in spite of the fact that in this hot summer break he probably had some free rooms. As it was past ten o'clock already, he pleaded with the owner to let them stay just that one night. Hearing this, his daughter, who had earlier sat next to him, covered her face with her hands and started crying. It embarrassed the owners, an elderly couple, and they conceded:

'Well, if it is only for one night, we might be able to accomodate you', but his daughter did not stop crying.

'Don't worry. We will stay here only for tonight, all right? Tomorrow we will find another place. . . . Don't cry. . . . '

But her sobbing only increased in intensity.

'Do you want to leave here and go somewhere else? . . . It is rather late. . . . '

For the first time she took notice and nodded.

Thus the three of them got again on the train which was to take them back to the area where they had lived. It was nearly eleven o'clock by then. They had no choice but to look for some cheap lodging house as there was not a single familiar house in the area to which he could turn. The children leaning against each other fell asleep from exhaustion and began snoring.

The train, with very few passengers in it, ran very fast through along the edge of the dark palace moat from which there blew a pleasantly moist evening breeze. How will you possibly be able to carry on living! – the expression of the face of K when he had said this . . . or the face of that policeman . . . but is this in fact all that important? . . .

'And what about the effect it has on the children?'

Well, yes. . . . That is terrible. . . . No mistake about that!
But today, the only thing that mattered to his children and to
his tired head and body was the rest which they badly
needed.[4]

The main appeal of this work, and of many others that followed
the same pattern, lay in presenting a portrait of a man whose
attempt to live according to the dictates of his own conscience
condemned his life to failure and transformed him into a social
outcast.

Itō Sei draws attention to the level of emotional complexity
expressed through the I-novel:

The autobiographical novel was the author's way of lamenting
the fate which had prevented him from becoming a respectable
businessman or store-owner or teacher, and which had deprived
him of a full rich life as a family man. At the same time, it was an
expression of the pride he felt in managing to keep alive by selling
what he wrote for a pittance and in thus avoiding enslavement to
the humiliating social system. Generally speaking writers portrayed themselves negatively, denying the conventions of home
and society, and in flight, and many of the novels of the period
convey a sense of righteousness and purity, which the author
experienced because he refused to become involved in the society
around him.[5]

The latter part of this quotation in particularly interesting in
exposing the concept, latent in Japanese thought, of a close affinity
between the social, or rather a-social attitudes of isolation or flight
and the positive moral value judgement ('righteousness and purity')
that is traditionally attached to it. In traditional Japanese thought,
mainly due to the influence of Buddhism, isolation, flight and
reclusiveness are almost synonymous with purity and stability. Itō
Sei, among others, suggests that the *bundan* writers' negative attitude
towards society, although partly influenced by the social and
political circumstances of life in modern Japan, had its roots in
traditionally Japanese modes of thought and behaviour.

Historically, flight from society was a commonly-occurring
pattern of life among intellectuals and artists and this may well be
attributable to the influence of Buddhism. On the one hand
Buddhism views the existing world and society as a place of

temporary abode for the soul in its migration through the Universe, a place full of evil and suffering, and suggests that peace of mind can be regained only by the abandonment of worldly affairs; on the other hand it tends to be self-centred as it concentrates on the individual search for peace and happiness and places little emphasis on a humanistic awareness of others.

Whereas Christianity displays a strong awareness of others and considers the performance of works on their behalf to be the ultimate aim, Buddhism tends to seek stability in breaking contact with others and by isolating the self sensually from the influence of the outside world. In addition, on the personal level, Buddhism influenced the individual's perception of life itself, because it viewed life as an evanescent and temporary state and offered the awareness of impermanence (*mu*) and death as the ultimate aspect of existence. The Buddhist notion of impermanence does not simply imply that life is short. By saying that not only man but all the objects in nature are constantly changing, it made human death into something relative and lessened its impact.

Catholicism rejects suicide because suicide is a denial of God. But the man who finds life itself evanescent, feels that fighting with others on the battleground of society and struggling for temporal happiness are meaningless. This attitude leads a man to abandon the world and seek stability in a simulated social vacuum, in the life of a recluse, or even to throw life away altogether.[6]

Simultaneously with the development of the Buddhist-influenced 'logic of negation'[7] and denial of the real world, the religious view of nature developed. Nature became an antithesis to the world of man, a harmonious entity, reminder of the impermanence of things yet permanent and limitless in space and time. Only by submerging himself in the natural world and submitting himself to its laws could man avoid the confusion and suffering of this world. Nature became a place of retreat where through a denial of worldly benefits man would learn the virtues of a pure and simple life and thus achieve peace of mind.

The ideal of the *yamazato* (mountain retreat) as a permanent dwelling place developed in the Kamakura (1182–1333) and Muromachi (1333–1615) periods and found its embodiment in such literary figures as Saigyō (1118–90), Kamo no Chōmei (1153–1216) and later Matsuo Bashō (1644–94). For medieval writers, living under the strictly controlled feudal system based on military power, the substantial problem was not how to write beautifully, but how to live while preserving the integrity of their conscience and be artistically creative at the same time. To achieve their aim they felt compelled to break their ties with the cultural élite, which was associated with authority and power, and seek refuge in nature and religion. The poet Saigyō abandoned his *samurai* status, left the court to travel widely and eventually settled as a priest in a temple in Takano and then in Ise. Kamo no Chōmei, also a court poet, fled into the mountains near Kyoto where he spent the rest of his days living in a primitive hut and writing up his thoughts in his famous work *Hōjōki* (1212) which expressed a Buddhist view of life. Matsuo Bashō, a famous haiku poet of the early Edo period, travelled all over Japan on foot leaving it to the country people and his literary friends to provide him with food.

This tendency to 'abandon the world' gave rise to what is termed recluse literature. It expressed an ideal of withdrawal from public life and rejected concern with society and politics, forming a model of behaviour which was basically escapist. The estrangement of the writers from the élite had two results. It created a tendency towards the formation of small exclusive groups of writers. As Katō Shūichi has pointed out, 'the "recluses" of the Muromachi period did not simply live alone in grass huts, but drank sake with others of their kind; they did not wander in the wilderness, but visited their fellows and travelled with them'.[8] Furthermore, as the centuries went by, this gradually imposed a limitation on the themes of literature, as the writers knew no other world but their own.

It may be considered one of the paradoxes of modern Japanese literature that in spite of its claims to modernity and deliberate efforts to break with the past, it was firmly rooted in traditional oriental thought, where the only reality is the reality of the self, in isolation from society; and it drew its spiritual strength from the centuries-old lyrical tradition of Japanese literature, where epic works were few and far between. Epics would have required a breadth of vision which the social recluses were not in a position to acquire or develop.

In Itō Sei's view, there is a fundamental link between the indigenous tradition and the modern I-novel. The I-novel continues the same pattern as these earlier forms of flight. The concept of self-denial, self-abandonment, profoundly linked with a sense of purity and righteousness, was an important element of the *tōbō dorei* mentality. The fatalistic and passive view of life was part of their mental inheritance which they carried over into modern life. It was inevitable that in the reality of modern Japan the flight assumed a different form. Now it was accomplished through the creation of the *bundan*, the only place where the artist could freely engage in experiments with modern thought; and it had to continue in close association with the publishing industry. The writers in flight had to rely on the publisher to feed them, as only the publisher would give them the opportunity to sell the literature which was carrying the information about their lives as fugitive slaves.

Although the form varied, the basic nature of the escape remained unchanged. The *bundan* writers limited their field of vision purposely – they concentrated on events in their own lives, on a small circle of friends, on their relationships with publishers and women. They consciously eliminated external influences in order to preserve their spiritual balance and self-integrity. Their lives became completely *bundan*-oriented as did their literature.[9]

In the escapist I-novel the *bundan* writers found a perfect medium of expression. It was the literary genre which was least bound by a contrived artistic form and which required least knowledge of the outside world. Engaged in the experiment of true living, the writers prided themselves both on the nature of the experiment, and on having the courage to announce their practice openly. Their aim was to confess the truth about themselves, about even the most painful and shameful aspects of human nature. Therefore, fiction to them was a meaningless, artificial form, which they instinctively rejected. In the opinion of many Japanese critics, the I-novel permitted authors to describe their human condition with a degree of truth unknown in Western literature at the time. The nature of their experiment, however, carried out in isolation from society, prevented them from finding a means of transcending their experience to create literature of a more universal character, as happened in the West. They created portraits of isolated individuals, of men in flight, who had little in common with other groups in society.

In such a context it is perhaps not surprising that history, politics or society do not generally enter modern Japanese literature. The writers who are aware of social reality, like Futabatei Shimei (see chapter 1), Shimazaki Tōson, Mori Ōgai or members of the Shirakaba group, are rather exceptional and as such will be discussed separately. The works of the others are submerged in a great nihilistic tradition, where any criticism of the world is expressed through the attitude of withdrawal.

In the world of the I-novel we witness a process which has occurred frequently in the course of Japanese history; in the encounter with a foreign thought system, the new does not supplant the old, but blends into the indigenous tradition and becomes 'japanised' in the process. And thus the encounter with nineteenth-century Western thought and literature gave rise to a uniquely Japanese form of modern literature in the shape of the I-novel.

Reflecting on the different characters of the two literary traditions, Japanese and Western (the classical nineteenth-century European novel serves as the model for comparison here), Itō Sei formulated an interesting theory in reference to the writer's relation to society in the respective cultures. While the Japanese writer is a *tōbō dorei*, a fugitive slave, the Western writer is in the position of a *kamen shinshi*, a gentleman in a mask.[10]

KAMEN SHINSHI

Compared with the Japanese writer he occupies a privileged position: he moves in the high social circles of the European salons; his art is appreciated as a valuable social asset and an inherent part of the cultural tradition of the nation; he fulfils the function of moralist and educator. But being accepted by the society, he has to pay the price of having to hide his private thoughts and emotions behind the mask of a gentleman. He cannot express his feelings openly and freely in literature as Japanese writers can. He can only express them through a fictional hero, who is part of a fictional structure, modelled by the writer on the image of the real society which surrounds him. Thus living in harmony with society, the European writer is continuously forced to wear a mask, both in his life and in his works. 'Bel-Ami or Maupassant, when leaving for a social gathering in formal dress, could not tell their reflections in the mirror from each other.'[11] And although, behind the mask, the writer went through the agony of the impostor conscious of the vulgarity and hypocrisy of the society in which he lived, he could hardly afford either to abandon it or to drop the mask. Even in nineteenth-century Russia, where the suppression of intellectual movements was similar to that in Japan, writers still belonged to the intelligentsia, had a definite sphere of social contacts, and were related to a whole system of cultural and moral values, which they could not abandon to write an autobiography in the Japanese style.

In the search for a rational and harmonious relation with the world, the Western writer encountered the inevitable conflict between his individual consciousness and society, and this sometimes led him ultimately to destruction. In Europe the latter usually took the form of insanity or escape into religion. Insanity brought destruction to such famous European writers as Strindberg, Maupassant, Nietzsche, Baudelaire and Poe; Tolstoy at the end of his life looked for salvation and redemption in religion, thus denying his own works.

The source of conflict between the individual and society lay in the spirit of positivism and Christianity, which shaped the historical development of Western societies. The Christian belief in love and self-control of one's natural desires, combined with the positivistic tradition in which man is viewed as a rational being who builds, analyses, discovers the causes of diseases and cures them, created a system within which all evil is ascribed to the individual's ego, which must be suppressed. This system cannot forgive man his own nature. A Western writer having inherited and being himself part of that cultural tradition, had to control, suppress or pervert his human desires. But when, in the long struggle with that tradition, the modern writer came to reveal the truth about man, it had to be hidden under the mask of fiction. The psychological novel of Western society was 'a masked ball' where the honest were not welcome. Because of its fictional structure, which constituted the writer's mask, the European novel also fulfilled a historical function, as it was only through careful observation of the surrounding reality and a detailed knowledge of his environment that the author was able to construct his models. Thus the novel thus became excellent material for the historian.

There was a very different situation in Japan. Here the novel became a device in the hands of social escapists, who preserved their lives from compromise by hiding in a literary guild and judging their hearts only according to the ethics of the guild. The merciless and cruel honesty with which they described their lives there was not hindered by feelings of shame or guilt. One reason, in Itō Sei's view, lay in their basically pagan mentality, free from the supervision of the Christian morality which dominated the West. Although most post-Meiji writers were familiar with the precepts of Christianity, it never became a practised ideology in the *bundan*. The writers never attempted to solve their human problems through God. Their view of the world never embraced Christianity as a transcendental system of universal and absolute values. In fact, most writers influenced by Christianity in their youth, only turned to literature after they had lost their faith. They remained fundamentally faithful to the indigenous Japanese view of the world where no transcendental principle exists. Japanese thought is traditionally concerned with the matters of this world. The affirmation of reality in this tradition derives from the perception of *mu* – the impermanence of all things – and from a conscious desire to live in harmony with Nature. This rationale does not encompass man as an integral component of society, but as a single particle of the Universe.

It is a constantly recurring concept in Itō Sei's works that at the root of the cultural difference between the West and East lies this contrast in their respective attitudes towards the self, which has subsequently produced different modes of thought and intellectual postures:

> People who are strongly aware of their own ego as well as the egoism of others, cooperate in a social contract whereby they voluntarily suppress it. Religion and democratic politics fulfil this function. A society where such a contract has been created operates smoothly. People who are not strongly aware of their ego cannot adapt their mutual relations accordingly, and that is why they accept the fact of organisation being imposed on them by an outside authority. In this situation an absolutist feudal system retains its power over a long period. . . . In the first type of society, the human conflict (*iwa*) rises in the heart of the restrained individual. Those aware of the conflict are led to mental destruction. In the second type of society such men abandon society and politics, and become social recluses; and here only one step separates them from suicide. The fact that in modern Europe there are many writers who have gone insane, and in Japan many who have committed suicide seems to be a manifestation of this tendency.[12]

Itō Sei's views in the area of comparative literary studies have been quoted at some length here not so much for his presentation of the Western cultural patterns, which seem rather perfunctory, but for the insight which they offer into the characteristic features of modern Japanese literature as it developed at the beginning of this century.

In the background of Japanese literature lies a fundamentally negative world-view and this, combined with the special way of life in the *bundan*, has tended to propel modern writers towards self-destruction (*hametsu*). *Hametsugata* is the term which Itō Sei used to describe those I-novelists whose basically escapist attitude had gradually transformed their lives into a self-annihilatory descent towards death.

HAMETSUGATA

Somewhere along the line which links Kasai Zenzō and Dazai Osamu, in the second half of the Taishō period, several important developments occurred in the *bundan* which marked out this path of the social escapists towards self-destruction. The first can be seen perhaps as a direct result of the principle of unity between the writer's life and his works, which reigned supreme in the *bundan*. In order to preserve that unity the writers felt compelled at some stage to begin to experiment with their lives so as to transform them into material suitable for description in I-novel terms and to fulfil the expectations of the I-novel reader.

The naturalistic canon of the I-novel made the author concentrate on the bleak aspects of human life. As Itō Sei once said, the privilege of writing the I-novel belonged to the underprivileged. The I-novelist believed himself to be more unhappy than most: deprived of his mother's love, betrayed by his wife, poverty stricken and in weak health, rejected by all, a social failure and outcast. Moreover, writers like Kasai Zenzō, Kamura Isota and Dazai Osamu strove to portray themselves in the above terms even though the reality of their lives, as witnessed by friends and family members, did not always conform to such a presentation. The spirit of the I-novel demanded from the author a constant focus on crisis or drama in his personal life:

Domestic strife, or the perils of a love affair, or sickness or bankruptcy punctuate the escapist's life with excitement. And the writer eventually reaches a point where he subconsciously welcomes these misfortunes. In the next stage he begins to act in such a way as to create them for himself. He takes positive steps to become involved in a dangerous and experimental love affair. And the reader enjoys his book all the more because it conveys a sense of impending peril. In this way a life of histrionics based on flight leads to destructive action.[13]

The element of histrionics in the lives of the Japanese I-novelists is observed and recognised by most Japanese literary scholars as being at the root of their self-destructive behaviour.[14] This theory of histrionic action (*engisetsu*) identifies a very unusual phenomenon in the literary world. As the writers, subconsciously perhaps, attempted to transform their lives into interesting reading material, they gradually began to live the lives of the heroes of their own works. In other words, they became victims of their own art, as their way of life became subject to the requirements of that art.

Thus the normal order of artistic creation, in which the artist, in very general terms, draws inspiration from his experience and transforms it into art, is being reversed in the case of the I-novelists. With them life itself becomes the artist's mould, and the distinction between art and life is obliterated. The writers became actors, who performed on the *bundan* stage plays about the lives of underprivileged I-novelists with the readers as their audience. By applying the rules of the stage to their own lives they initiated a sequence of events in the course of which they destroyed themselves.[15]

In Hirano Ken's view, this self-destructive process reveals a basic antinomy inherent in the I-novel world between the I-novel as a form of art and the artist's life. In the I-novel situation the concept of crisis in life becomes the sole inspiration for art. And the writers who acknowledge the supremacy of art over life are led from one crisis to another on a path of decline which eventually ends in premature death through illness or suicide.[16]

Death often becomes the only way of escape from the impossible conditions of life which they have themselves created. It brings to an end the irreversible process of disintegration to which their art bears witness. Death is the final gesture which suitably concludes the histrionic life of the I-novelist and his art.

On the other hand, those writers who chose to introduce a measure of rational control over their lives, like Shiga Naoya, were effectively faced with the choice of either abandoning the I-novel or stopping writing altogether.

The histrionic attitude of the I-novelists developed partly in response to the expectations of the readers. In spite of the fact that the *watakushi shōsetsu* was a specifically *bundan* creation concerned with the vicissitudes and emotional problems of the professional writer's life and was difficult to appreciate by those who did not belong to the *bundan*, nevertheless it acquired a considerable readership during the first half of the twentieth century, especially among young Japanese intellectuals. The reader of the I-novel, being himself bound to real society through his job and family, 'found happiness in getting intimate with the life of the author who had escaped from this corrupt world and lived an ideal life in freedom and solitude', where there was no need for submission or compromise. In a sense the I-novel built up an image of the writer as the only free human being in Japanese society. It presented an ideal moral attitude towards life, which the reader, especially when young, hoped to follow himself.[17]

Paradoxical though it may seem, it was because of that assured readership that the writers, aware of the commercial value of their works, felt obliged to continue writing the I-novels while acting out the lives of the miserable novelists which they themselves created. Otherwise their works, whose literary success depended entirely on the authenticity of the narrative, would lose their value. Itō Sei describes the phenomenon as 'commercialistic histrionics':

> no attempt at flight or escape, no matter how seriously it is conceived and begun, can sustain itself in any pure form where capitalistic journalism prevails, and . . . there is a grave danger that escapism will lead to commercialistic histrionics that have nothing to do with the original objective.[18]

The tendency towards the commercialisation of the I-novel became particularly pronounced after the First World War, when the fast growth of the literary market accompanied by a greatly expanded readership transformed the I-novel into a desirable market commodity. The writers could no longer remain immune to the fact that their works brought them popularity and financial rewards which were rapidly changing the reality of their lives. To satisfy the demands of the market they began writing numerous I-novels that had little to do with the original search for truth or freedom. The pure world of the I-novel, supported by the élitist consciousness of the artist who was prepared to ignore society's rewards for the sake of his art, was heading towards decline.

Kamura Isota, mentioned earlier among the *hametsugata* writers, was the man who, to use the phrase of Fukuda Tsuneari, 'buried the

I-novel with him when he died'.[19] Itō Sei also tends to consider Kamura Isota as a writer in whose works the Japanese I-novel reached its apogee. His writing represents this later phase of the I-novel, at a time when the artist's integrity was threatened by the commercial success of his work. The special value of Kamura's novels lies in the fact that he touched on the subject of the artist's professional snobbery, which until then had been a taboo in naturalistic literature. The writers would confess with a feeling of shame or self-disgust all the misery of their lives, they would admit their lack of success in the eyes of society, but they would never attack what was their secret pride, their final fortress behind which they felt secure – their belief in the artist as a superior being. They saw their art as a religious discipline and themselves as priests in its service. These two concepts of the sanctity of art and the superiority of artists were to compensate them for their failure in real life.

Kamura Isota, a pupil of Kasai Zenzō, went a step further. He not only described in a typical naturalistic fashion the weakness and ugliness of himself as a human being, but went deeper into the problem of professional pride and exposed it as a mutation of the desire for wordly success. There is a revealing paragraph in one of his novels, *Shinzen kekkon* (A Marriage before God), where the novelist receives the news of his story having been accepted by a leading magazine and shouts '*Nippon ichi ni natta!*' ('I became the best in Japan'). Until Kamura Isota there was no such deliberate attempt to denigrate the artist's feeling of moral superiority by presenting it merely as a form of *risshin shusse* (worldly advancement) ideology. With an almost masochistic persistence Kamura delved into the feelings of guilt and self-recrimination, which became the source of his own art. He is acknowledged as a writer who in drawing out all the ugliness of his guilty conscience achieved the 'beauty of absolute truth' in his works. Through Kamura Isota the I-novel described a full circle by confessing in its final stages the shame and ugliness of being a professional writer.

Dazai Osamu is often considered the last, most illustrious, victim of the I-novel method. It is even suggested that Itō Sei formulated his theory of the self-destructive I-novel with Dazai in mind. In his life, Dazai seems to have gone through all the characteristic stages that led from social escape towards self-destruction: a broken relationship with his home and family, a life of dissipation in Tokyo, material and psychological insecurity, ruined health, drugs, debts and several attempts at suicide and double suicide. Dazai's successful suicide in 1948 (followed a year later by the suicide of his pupil and friend Tanaka Hidemitsu)marks an end to a whole epoch in the modern Japanese literary tradition. In the new post-war era of affluence and political freedom, the *tōbō dorei* mentality gave way to new concerns calling for a re-definition of literary values and of the role of literary men in society, but these are outside the scope of the present study.

Dazai Osamu's works no longer follow the naturalistic commandment of strict adherence to the realities of life. While earlier writers like Iwano Hōmei, Tayama Katai or Chikamatsu Shūkō wrote faithful accounts of their lives, from about the time of Kasai Zenzō and Uno Kōji an element of fiction had been gradually introduced into the I-novel, and from the beginning of the Shōwa period it became a common practice among the I-novelists. Dazai's novels are largely fiction written in the I-novel spirit. What this means is that although the events described in the novels did not necessarily take place in Dazai's life, the novels as a whole essentially reflect the reality of his life and his feelings at the time, and as such they were accepted by critics and readers alike as confessional I-novels.

His method is clearly visible in a work like *Villon's Wife* (1947), a story about the disintegration of a writer's life as told by his wife. To repay the money her husband has stolen from a restaurant owner the wife begins working in the same restaurant, thus finding for the first time some stability for her own life. The novel ends in the following way:

> God, if you exist, show yourself to me! Towards the end of the New Year season I was raped by a customer. It was raining that night, and it didn't seem likely that my husband would appear. I got ready to go, even though one customer was still left. I picked up the boy, who was sleeping in a corner of the back room, and put him on my back. 'I would like to borrow your umbrella again', I said to the madam.
>
> 'I've got an umbrella. I'll take you home', said the last customer, getting up as if he meant it. He was short, thin man about twenty-five, who looked like a factory worker. It was the first time he had come to the restaurant since I started working there.
>
> 'It's very kind of you, but I am used to walking by myself.'
>
> 'You live a long way off, I know. I come from the same

neighbourhood. I'll take you back. Bill, please.' He had only had three glasses and didn't seem particularly drunk.

We boarded the streetcar together and got off at my stop. Then we walked in the falling rain side by side under the same umbrella through the pitch-black streets. The young man, who up to this point hadn't said a word, began to talk in a lively way. 'I know all about you. You see, I'm a fan of Mr Otani's and I write poetry myself. I was hoping to show him some of my work before long, but he intimidates me so.'

We had reached my house. 'Thank you very much', I said. 'I'll see you again at the restaurant.'

'Goodbye', the young man said, going off into the rain.

I was wakened in the middle of the night by the noise of the front gate being opened. I thought that it was my husband returning, drunk as usual, so I lay there without saying anything.

A man's voice called, 'Mrs Otani, excuse me for bothering you.'

I got up, put on the light, and went to the front entrance. The young man was there, staggering so badly he could scarcely stand.

'Excuse me, Mrs Otani. On the way back I stopped for another drink and, to tell the truth, I live at the other end of town, and when I got to the station the last streetcar had already left. Mrs Otani, would you please let me spend the night here? I don't need any blankets or anything else. I'll be glad to sleep here in the front hall until the first streetcar leaves tomorrow morning. If it wasn't raining I'd sleep outdoors somewhere in the neighbourhood, but it's hopeless with this rain. Please let me stay.'

'My husband isn't at home, but if the front hall will do, please stay.' I got the two torn cushions and gave them to him.

'Thanks very much. Oh, I've had too much to drink', he said with a groan. He lay down just as he was in the front hall, and by the time I got back to bed I could already hear his snores.

The next morning at dawn without ceremony he took me.

That day I went to the restaurant with my boy as usual, acting as if nothing had happened. My husband was sitting at a table reading a newspaper, a glass of liquor beside him. I thought how pretty the morning sunshine looked, sparkling on the glass.

'Isn't anybody here?' I asked. He looked up from his paper. 'The boss hasn't come back yet from marketing. The madam was in the kitchen just a minute ago. Isn't she there now?'

'You didn't come last night, did you?'

'I did come. It's got so that I can't get to sleep without a look at my favourite waitress's face. I dropped in after ten but they said you had just left.'

'And then?'

'I spent the night here. It was raining so hard.'

'I may be sleeping here from now on.'

'That's a good idea, I suppose.'

'Yes, that's what I'll do. There's no sense in renting the house forever.'

My husband didn't say anything but turned back to his paper. 'Well, what do you know. They're writing bad things about me again. They call me a fake aristocrat with Epicurean leanings. That's not true. It would be more correct to refer to me as an Epicurean in terror of God. Look! It says here that I'm a monster. That's not true, is it? It's a little late, but I'll tell you now why I took the five thousand yen. It was so that I might give you and the boy the first happy New Year in a long time. That proves I'm not a monster, doesn't it?'

His words didn't make me especially glad. I said, 'There's nothing wrong with being a monster, is there? As long as we can stay alive.'[20]

Reading a novel like *Villon's Wife* one becomes immediately aware of the change in the writer's attitude to life that occurred in the I-novel during the later stage of its development. Here the confidence of the earlier I-novelists, the joy of rebellion against social norms, is transformed into a fear of this freedom. The writer becomes aware of the de-humanising consequences of his self-centred search, which makes him trample over the unhappiness of his family, throws him into the depths of loneliness and despair, and brings confrontation with death.

Dazai's works present a crystallisation of the mental state of a writer faced with the tragic reality of his life, which becomes even more unbearable as he attributes it to his own action:

All my unhappiness is a result of my vice. . . . Am I, as it is commonly said, an egoist? Or am I, on the contrary, too timid? I myself don't know for sure. Anyway, as I seem to be vice personified, I make myself endlessly unhappy and I have no way to stop.[21]

These words of the protagonist of *No Longer Human* (*Ningen shikkaku*, 1948), Dazai's last major work, convey a sense of grief and self-recrimination and this deeply moves Japanese readers who traditionally find humanity and beauty in unhappiness. 'He was an angel' says the bar attendant about the protagonist in the last line of the novel.

On the other hand the appeal which this type of novel has for the reader comes from a gradual realisation that the everyday life rejected by the writer contains elements – home, family, friends – which are necessary to human happiness. A man who cuts himself off from all this is bound to be so lonely that he becomes incapable of continuing to live. The reader, on the other hand, comes to treasure his own happiness.

Dazai's novels reflect a change of emphasis in the I-novel. What Itō Sei defines as a horizontal description of reality (relationships with the surrounding society – friends, women, family, publishers – even though portrayed in the negative convention of flight) in the works of the earlier I-novelists gave way to a vertical concern with the meaning of life, death, Good and Evil.[22] Among the self-destructive I-novelists the comprehension of life occurs through the process of descent into death. The I-novel which began as a chronicle of flight from society became a pure search for the meaning of life; at the same time the original rebellion against society was transformed into a descent towards death and self-destruction.

CONCLUSION

The Japanese practice of the writer revealing his own ego precisely because it is disgusting and shameful is quite different from the European tradition of disguising the ego in order to preserve its integrity. Out of the method of confession the Japanese created a special type of modern literature whose literary reality and success depended entirely on a symbiotic relationship with the author's own life.

The I-novelists lived in a special environment which has been compared to a religious monastery, where the monks, cut off from the real world, devote themselves to the practice of an ascetic discipline, or to a *yakuza* community. *Yakuza* were members of a criminal underworld which possessed its own strong moral code of practice (*jingi*). In spite of their criminal record, there persists in popular literature a romantic image of a *yakuza* – a strong and honest man, whose sincerity of motive brings him into conflict with legitimate society, deprives him of the happiness of a home and family as he cannot afford any emotional ties with the outside world, and abandons him to his lonely journey through life. The analogy between a *yakuza* group and the *bundan* is built on the superficial resemblance of the two communities: both represent small exclusive worlds on the margins of social life, based on ideologies that clashed with the ideology of the surrounding legitimate society. The members of both worlds express a similar awareness of being 'men of the shadows', social outcasts destined to spend their lives in solitude and unhappiness. There is however an aspect of that analogy with the *yakuza* which would not please the *bundan* man, as it casts a shadow on the 'modern way of life' in the *bundan*. The *yakuza* moral code and its social structure based on the absolute loyalty in *oyabun* and *kobun* relations clearly represent a feudal type of organisation. As though to confirm a similar tendency in the *bundan*, there is an article by Hirano Ken on Kamura Isota and Kasai Zenzō, where he describes the relations between the two writers as obviously feudal, and where he refers to the *hametsugata* novelists and their ideas of establishing themselves through art by sacrificing the happiness of their families as 'redolent of pre-modern times'.[23]

Due to the special relation between art and life in the *bundan*, the writers found themselves on an endlessly repetitive circular track from which the way to the present was blocked off. As Itō Sei pointed out, if they tried to progress forward from there they faced death; if they tried to live and retreated backwards, they were faced with their old enemy – the real world, and the only means of breaking out of that was revolution. Japanese thought moves only in the sphere of real life. It does not have the convention of God to which it can look for salvation. And as writers had renounced also the art of mask and disguise, they were guided only by principles of death or revolution.[24]

Before considering the writers who chose the revolutionary way to self-destruction, some mention should be made of those few who, though they defied authority and tradition, nevertheless attempted to seek harmony with the world surrounding them.

4 In Search of Logic and Social Harmony

During the same period that witnessed the development of the *bundan*, there were in Japan great writers whose lives and works placed them outside the main *bundan* current. Due to the particular circumstances of their lives, these writers, unlike the inhabitants of the *bundan*, remained aware of the outside world and sought to establish the basis for a rational and harmonious existence within society. Consequently their works provided modern Japanese literature with perhaps the only examples of social perspective and a critical approach to the problem of the relationship between the individual and society in modern Japan. Shimazaki Tōson, Natsume Sōseki, Mori Ōgai and also the members of the Shirakaba group, with Shiga Naoya as its main representative, belong to this category in spite of the great variations in their individual positions.

Their search for social harmony was, as will be seen, not necessarily successful in personal terms, but their works found a permanent place in the history of Japanese literature. History has played one of its ironical jokes in that it is these writers, criticised and ignored by the *bundan* as literary dilettanti, who are the most read and best loved by Japanese readers even today, while the corpus of naturalistic literature has been relegated to oblivion. One reason for this popularity, apart from the undisputedly high artistic quality of their novels, may come from the fact that these writers provided models of social behaviour in which the individual could relate himself to society in a positive and constructive manner without destroying himself.

The presentation in this chapter of the character and the quality of the effort towards harmony made by Japanese writers will mainly follow Itō Sei's line of argument, as he was one of the most prominent exponents of the *chōwa* (harmony) theory in Japanese literature.

SHIMAZAKI TŌSON (1872–1943)

Among the *chōwa*-type writers Shimazaki Tōson occupies a peculiar position. He is 'a *bundan* inhabitant who did not abandon his link with society'. For a *bundan-jin* it was an unusual attitude to adopt – remaining a member of the feudal family system, maintaining contacts with relatives, and reconciling oneself with the old, meaningless, inhuman way of life. The fact that Tōson had readers outside the literary world seems to have been due to this conciliatory character of his mode of thought.

This attitude towards life enabled Tōson to express his consciousness as a modern man within the old framework of the family system without destroying himself. In Itō Sei's view, he performed a trick, of which no-one else was capable, combining peacefully and harmoniously the consciousness of a modern literary man with the traditional structure of Japanese society. The essence of Tōson's works lies precisely in this compromising attitude towards the social order, and it is his style that reflects it perhaps most clearly. In discarding the old order many of his contemporaries also abandoned its idiom, but Tōson made it into his forte.[1]

According to Itō Sei, Tōson's style, which reached its full maturity in his later works, from *Ie* on, is a unique phenomenon in modern Japanese literature:

Tōson's style during this period strikes me as being a prose rendering of Japanese *aisatsu*, the approach to and vocabulary of everyday 'civilities'. When a man learns on going to collect a debt that the money is not forthcoming, he may protest at great length, appealing to reason, to right of claim, to promises made. Or he may sit quietly in front of the debtor and suggest, laconically, circumlocutiously, that he too has to make a living, that he has his own honour to maintain. There can be not doubt that, in Japanese society, the latter approach will prove the more effective. The structure of Japanese society is such that reason and demonstrated proof count for much less than the pressure that derives from the individual's relation to his surroundings, from the necessity of saving face and preserving appearances. In this sort of society rational or realistic expression is effective only among the intellectual élite, in all the other vast strata of society peopled by masses it is language at once forceful and indirect, language that oppresses through insinuation, that is most telling.

And this is the secret that Tōson learned from the dynamics of the languages of *aisatsu*, as it is used in Japanese society at large.[2]

Tōson's ability to attract so many readers would be impossible to account for without considering the matter of his style. Whereas other writers of the period including Katai, Shūsei, Hōmei, had difficulties in selling their works in large numbers, Tōson's huge popularity with the general public never flagged.

In his essay 'Kindai nihonjin no hassō no shokeishiki', Itō Sei draws an interesting parallel between Tōson's style and his life. Tōson was born in Magome, Nagano-ken, to a well-known family. But at the age of ten he left home and grew to manhood among relatives, having to depend for the necessities of life on the hospitality of his hosts. This rigorous upbringing and the consciousness of being a dependant determined his style. The Japanese he spoke from day to day was the language one uses to a superior, to the master of the house. The language of propriety, of civility, the manner of speaking which enabled one to show deference to a superior while asserting himself was Tōson's mode of self-expression.[3]

There is only one short period in Tōson's life, when he was relatively independent, encumbered only by his wife and child. It corresponds to the period when he started his career as a prose writer – the period between his first collection *Chikumagawa no suketchi* (1900) and his first novel *Hakai* (1906). The collection, which is a kind of preparatory exercise for a novel, is written in lucid, realistic prose. Since Tōson was training himself to become a realist during this period, the style of his first novel *Hakai* is roughly the same. The novel was a remarkably successful attempt at using the colloquial language; it was recognised as the first naturalistic novel in Japan, and it determined the prose style to be used in Japanese novels for years afterwards.

But after Tōson reached the age of forty, the conditions of his life changed. He was obliged to help his own family, which in economic terms had declined disastrously, and to save his elder brother, whose business failure had led him into crime. Also about this time, after his wife's death, he began having an affair with his niece, his brother's daughter. If the affair had been exposed, it would have meant social ruin, and Tōson was afraid. There is even evidence that his brother, who sensed what was happening, was continuously asking Tōson for money – a kind of blackmail. At this point in his life

Tōson wrote *Shinsei*, which is an uncamouflaged confession of the affair. Temptation, feelings of guilt, and fear of social sanctions are the theme of the novel. When Tayama Katai, a close friend, read the novel, he could not help but predict that Tōson would commit suicide. But Akutagawa Ryūnosuke, a writer much younger than Tayama, is quoted as having said after reading *Shinsei*: 'There has never been a hypocrite like Shimazaki Tōson', and according to Itō Sei his view proved to be more accurate. Tōson wrote *Shinsei* with the intention of securing his position in society, breaking off the affair with his niece once and for all and putting an end to his brother's extortion:

> In modern Japanese society matters of love or scandal, or money, do not exist purely as problems in themselves. Invariably they are tightly interwoven not so much in social as in familial relationships, and Tōson's own position was a typical example. Difficulties encountered in such a society are resolved, not by reason or rationality, but by face: someone is sacrificed through the application of indirect pressure, and by interring the victim in grave after grave the family honour is maintained and the individual involved preserves himself. Tōson's attempt to extricate himself from his predicament was a subtle variation on this traditional method.[4]

Tōson's fear of society and his willingness to sacrifice his niece are only thinly disguised in the form of a confessional novel, and Akutagawa noticed this. Tōson merely borrowed the outer form of the confessional novel which was accepted as the modern man's mode of expression and was using it as a means of applying indirect pressure and appealling to face. But Itō Sei comes strongly to the defence of Tōson's method. However much it may have been criticised by *bundan* writers and critics, this was the only method which permitted Tōson to express himself fully without destroying his family ties. His works create a picture of a full man who has a strong desire to live in harmony with the world at the same time as being cunning enough to preserve himself and his miserable life.

In Itō Sei's view Tōson's position in Japanese literature and his achievement are unique. The naturalistic realism of Tayama Katai's kind was narrow, shortsighted and valid only within the boundaries of the *bundan*. On the other hand, in Japanese society at large, any effort aiming at self-fulfilment in a rational manner inevitably led either to revolutionary action involving destruction of others (as was shown by the case of proletarian literature), or to the destruction of the rationally-conceived self (e.g. Mori Ōgai or Natsume Sōseki). Yet Shimazaki Tōson was able to accomplish the miracle: his mode of thought, revealed in his style, 'was neither purely rational, nor meekly submissive to the old conventions, but proceeded along the middle ground without destroying either side, and yet enabled the author to assert himself to gain fulfilment', and there lies his strength.[5]

Mori Ōgai and Natsume Sōseki present a very different case. They never belonged to the *bundan* and throughout their lives firmly opposed its artistic ideas. Both their established social position and the fictional character of their literary works placed them outside the *bundan* in the narrow sense. As they became famous, in the readers' eyes they were naturally a part of the literary establishment but to the contemporary *bundan*, so dogmatic about the close naturalistic relationship between life and art, Ōgai and Sōseki because of the circumstances of their lives and the type of literature they wrote, remained compromisers and dilettanti. It is possible to regard their position as closer to the European *kamen shinshi*, to use Itō Sei's phrase, than to the typical *bundanjin*.

Itō Sei emphasised the connection between, on the one hand, the non-autobiographical character of their works and their opposition to the naturalistic method of description, and on the other the non-escapist quality of their lives. He feels that their awareness of the outside world and the attempt to view it rationally as displayed in their works were the result of their privileged social position.

Thus Itō Sei's parallel becomes complete: the life of the *tōbō dorei* encourages the confessional novel (*hōki* ——➤ *tōbō dorei* mentality ——➤ I-novel),[6] while the life of *kamen shinshi* prevents it:

chōwa (harmony) ——➤ *gensei ishiki* (awareness of the world) ——➤ possibility of fiction (or form, *zōkei* in Itō Sei's term)

Life in society creates the need for a fictional structure in the world of art.

MORI ŌGAI (1862–1922)

Mori Ōgai provides the closest example to the *kamen shinshi* position in Japanese society. Itō Sei describes him as having lived his creative life in European-like fashion, with the status of a gentleman and the necessity to associate with the men of the world who surrounded him.[7]

What is being referred to here is the fact that by birth, education and career Mori Ōgai was a representative of the ruling bureaucratic class. This secured him a position as an army official which he held until his resignation at the age of fifty-eight. He was a medical officer of high rank and inevitably had to associate with his superiors in the military and with government officials who upheld the Meiji order. Writing was only his spare time activity. He never wrote autobiographical novels in the *watakushi shōsetsu* tradition, thus fulfilling the other condition of a *kamen shinshi*. His works remind one more, writes Itō Sei, of Flaubert, who described the self only under the disguise of another man. His literary style was lucid and logical; his works were constructed within the sphere of authentically objective phenomena, and assumed a shape which in principle was in accordance with the positive stream in modern European literature.[8]

Ōgai's opposition to the I-novel *bundan* came from the two different sources of his education: first, the feudal *samurai* tradition and, secondly, the European scientific and literary tradition (in the 1880s Ōgai spent four years in Europe where he studied Western medicine and became well acquainted with, and greatly influenced by, the thought and literature of the period). The implications of the merger of these two great cultural traditions in Ōgai's life are far too complex to examine exhaustively here, but a few points should perhaps be mentioned to illuminate the position he took as a writer.

His *samurai* upbringing tied him to the oligarchic, autocratic Meiji government; it also imbued him with a strong sense of social responsibility and appreciation for traditional Japanese values. The West to him symbolised science and a logical, systematic way of thinking, and rationality in social relations. Ōgai viewed Japan as a country undergoing the process of modernisation[9] and saw his responsibility to be to enlighten the public while taking into account both the national tradition and Western ideas. In that sense he continued the intellectual tradition of the Japanese enlightenment, representing the group of thinkers who tried to instil into Japanese society the rationality that would enable every citizen to enjoy the dignity which was man's birthright.

Ōgai came back from Germany greatly impressed by the degree of freedom the individual enjoyed there. In an early work written soon after his return (*Maihime*, The Dancer, 1980) he describes how in the atmosphere of freedom the hero became aware of his own self. The essence of this awareness lay in recognising the weak points of the self and trying to find rational solutions to the problem of supplying the deficiencies. Ōgai's individualism was directed towards seeking the ways in which the individual could relate himself rationally to his surroundings. Within the framework of a rational relation to society the individual would be able to display his intellectual will and energy, thus aiming at building a harmonious self.

Ōgai disapproved of the egoistic despair of the naturalists, of their attitude of negation and escape, which eventually led them to self-destruction. In opposition to their concept of man ruled by instinct and passion, he set his image of man controlled by reason; he opposed their concept of the individual maintaining balance through negation or *mu* awareness, offering instead his positive way of thinking. *Vita Sexualis* (1909) may serve as an example of how his open rationality was as unacceptable to the establishment as the naturalists' rebellion against social mores. Ōgai described there, in the form of a retired university professor's confession, his youthful sexual experiences and desires, which he overcame in order to become a 'real intellectual'. An immediate prohibition of sale followed the appearance of the book, as it described too honestly the sexual life of a young person.

Ōgai was often criticised, however, by his fellow writers, who argued that although advocating reason, harmony and self-control, he relied too much on the traditional family values of self-discipline and authority. *Kamen* (Mask, 1909), regarded as Ōgai's most obviously anti-naturalistic work, argues in favour of wearing a 'mask' over one's emotional life – self-restraint, observance of the proper civilities of social life and refraining from causing needless worries to those in one's immediate environment constitute a mask which helps to transcend the ugliness and weakness of instinctive human beings. The mask fulfils its role in modern Japan by helping men to live actively and significantly, in accordance with the dictates of wisdom. Thus Ōgai's mode of thought even in his early works represents modern logic and rationality operating within the old feudal ethical code. A reflection of this can be traced to a certain extent in Ōgai's style. He had been a great lover of the classics in his youth and these tastes led him from time to time to garnish his prose with ornate trappings from the classical and Chinese styles. His ornamented, elegantly polite style, close to the vague, feudal *aisatsu* style of Tōson and running against the *bundan* literary ideas of the time, expressed the author's intention of achieving a 'conciliatory compromise' with society.[10] He could not afford to discard society in the way the naturalists did. Rational thought differs in its character from the passive contemplation of those who abandoned the world (*gensei hōkisha*), and it becomes useless if it does not appeal to the real society. It may have been the same desire to be socially useful that impelled him into government service, despite his outstanding literary talents as translator, poet, novelist and critic. An army career was in Meiji Japan one of the highways of rising in the world and it had attracted many socially-minded writers, for example, Futabatei Shimei, who in his youth had sought to enter the military academy.

Yet having placed himself voluntarily in the world of army officials, Ōgai was faced with a psychological dilemma: he was oscillating between the old precepts of a feudal *bushi* which he had inherited through his birth and education, and the individualism of a modern man. As has been shown in the example of *Kamen*, the old precepts were consciously converted into modern equivalents within his system of logic. And perhaps, 'so far as this conversion was possible, he saw more chance for peace for himself in being a military official than in being a member of the *bundan*, the world of those who practised irrationality'.[11]

Nevertheless, he was aware of the threat which the bureaucratic machine posed to his responsibilities as a modern man, to his fight for the greater freedom of the individual. He apprehended the danger of becoming, as a bureaucrat, a puppet deprived of its own will. His predicament became particularly acute from about the time of the Kōtoku affair, which clearly manifested the 'irrational' course Meiji Japan had taken. He could not stop himself from viewing the world rationally and thus could not remain indifferent to socialist thought, but at the same time he could not criticise the Meiji order *per se* without sacrificing his own position. Ultimately he decided to withdraw from open battle with the contemporary world and adopted the attitude of resignation (*tachinokase*), which is clearly expressed in *Kano yō ni* (As if), a short novel written in the last year of Meiji. The hero of *Kano yō ni* is a resigned young man educated in Europe who, when accused by a friend of not being involved, reveals that he no longer believes in the ethical norms of his society. However, he considers rejection of society as a meaningless and

unsatisfactory way to personal happiness, and chooses as the only
practical solution, behaving *as if* he did believe in the system, thus
suggesting that there is no way out for an honest man in a society like
the Japanese. Asked why he does not fight, his only answer is an
outburst of laughter, expressing his feeling of helplessness.

In the later part of his life Ōgai turned to historical novels and
biographies and these are usually considered to be of much higher
literary value than his works of the previous period. The world he
created here was of a pre-Meiji order, and he found he could convey
his observations and thoughts more objectively and realistically.
But his interest remained the same: the conflict between the
expectations of the individual and his duties towards society. This
was the conflict which presented the most serious issue in Ōgai's
own life. Itō Sei argues that judging by the form of Ōgai's thought
he should have seen the world clearly in terms of the relation of the
individual to the social order. But, at bottom, Ōgai's sentiment
about life had its roots deep in feudal society, and he sensed a
congenial quality in the logicality, positivism, and at the same time
the old style stoicism of the world of military officialdom. It was
from the fictionalisation of this nostalgia, which ran deep in his life,
that his historical novels like *Izawa Ranken* and others were
created.[12]

Izawa Ranken is a chronicle of the life of a physician and writer
living under the feudal system. The analogy with Ōgai's life is so
striking that the work found an approval even among confirmed
naturalists like Katai, who remarked: 'For the first time Ōgai has
described himself.'[13] Despite this acclaim voiced by a *bundan* writer,
Izawa Ranken is, in Itō's opinion, a perfect novel from the European
point of view. It expresses the writer's ego in a rational manner
under the disguise of a hero. It also conveys the author's anxieties,
but only within the framework permitted by social conventions and
history, thus saving the living author from destruction.

In spite of the rationality which permeated his thought and
works, or perhaps precisely because of it, Ōgai remained torn by
doubts, lonely and isolated. From about the mid-Taishō period, he
began increasingly to view his historical novels as a 'pastime' (*asobi*),
and to assume the attitude of a passive observer towards the world
around him. To Itō Sei he represents a case which proves that in
Japanese society 'where neither social, familial, nor business
relationships are rationally orientated, no attempt on the
individual's part to assert himself rationally from beginning to end

can hope to succeed, not if he hopes at the same time to lead a balanced, harmonious life'.[14]

NATSUME SŌSEKI (1867–1916)

In Itō Sei's spectrum of the Japanese literary scene, Natsume Sōseki is placed somewhere near Mori Ōgai. Like Ōgai he stood aloof from the mainstream of the literary world of the day, and like Ōgai he had the privileged social position of a gentleman (*shinshi*) although in his case it was acquired through his status as a famous writer surrounded by many followers.[15] Sōseki never held a government post; he resigned from his professorship at Tokyo Imperial University to become a staff member of the Tokyo *Asahi Shimbun* (Asahi Newspaper) and continued to live from his writing to the end of his life;[16] he also refused the many honours which the establishment wished to bestow on him, which seems to suggest that he felt rather less comfortable than Ōgai in the skin of a 'gentleman'.

The tendency towards withdrawal, which in a sense reminds one of Ōgai's 'resignation', is clearly manifested in Sōseki's literary career as a novelist, which started after his return from Europe in 1903. His early works (*Wagahai wa neko de aru*, I am a Cat, 1905; *Botchan*, 1906, etc.) can be compared to realistic European literature in their method of description and the element of social criticism which they contained. The hero is a living member of society, fully described, and his thoughts and deeds are logically explainable. The reader therefore does not require any 'preparatory' knowledge to grasp the meaning of the novel, as he did in the case of *watakushi shōsetsu*.

Natsume Sōseki and the group of young thinkers and writers that surrounded him represented that part of the intelligentsia among which 'reason' began to hold sway at the end of Meiji. They were young men from well-off families who suffered no material hardship, and they were able to detach themselves sufficiently from tradition and social contracts to consider their lives rationally.[17] That such rational re-orientation of one's life was not an easy task to perform in practical terms is not surprising. In a memorandum which he wrote in English, Sōseki gave expression to this resistance of the environment to the impact of his rational thought, describing his university professor colleagues as 'beasts'. At home he flew into violent rages so often that his wife became convinced that he was insane.

Throughout his life Sōseki suffered from the dual character of his existence, from having to maintain the life of a 'gentleman' and public figure on the one hand, while being fully aware of the brutal undercurrent of human behaviour on the other. One can get a glimpse into his inner anxieties in the collection of short stories *Yume jūya* (Ten Nights' Dreams, 1908) describing the author's dreams on ten successive nights. *Michigusa* (Grass on the Wayside, 1915), the only autobiographical novel he wrote, came from his efforts to preserve his inner harmony.

Sōseki's final withdrawal from public life and his decision to concentrate exclusively on his writing may perhaps be seen as an admission of the incompatibility of his aims and the irrational course of development being taken by the Japanese State. In 1916 he wrote:

In modern Japan politics is politics and nothing else. And thought is thought and nothing else. These two things exist in the same society in complete isolation from each other. There is no understanding or communication between them. And when an idea appears which discovers the link between the two, it does so only to be suppressed in the form of the prohibition of sale.[18]

Disillusioned with the State, Sōseki turned in his later works (*Mon*, The Gate, 1910; *Sore kara*, And Then, 1909; *Kōjin*, The Wayfarer, 1913; *Kokoro*, 1914, etc.) away from direct social criticism towards individualism. The individual becomes the stronghold of moral values, since the State has not much to do with them. Sōseki exhibits a profound concern with the individual of a moral and religious nature; he denounces the superficial quality of Western civilisation, which reduced the individual to the role of a slave of his own ego, making him abandon his own inner ethical standards in favour of a superficially understood notion of liberty and equality and thus only detaching him from real happiness. In *Meian* (Light and Shade, 1916), Sōseki's last and most mature book, he expressed his doubts within the framework of the man–woman relationship, saying that real family life becomes almost impossible as the modern husband and wife lose the capacity to serve each other. From about the time *Meian* appeared, Sōseki began to comprehend with great clarity that the ideal of self-assertion meant not merely battle with the external elements that oppressed the individual but also unavoidably involved a conscious or aggressive conquest of others in an attempt to extend one's own self limitlessly. In *Meian* the ugliness of the self in its unappeasable desire for conquest is exposed.[19]

The dangers of self-assertion were sensed by naturalist writers as well. Natsume Sōseki and, slightly later in the early Shōwa period, Kamura Isota, using different methods, expressed similar feelings about the ugliness of human nature. Sōseki's fiction and Kamura's chronicle of his life exposed with disgust human egoism, envy, hate, meanness, servility and aggression – qualities which rule people's lives and relationships. But while the naturalists tied their views closely to their own particular experience which they never analysed in more universal terms, Sōseki's rational thought and his deep analytical insight revealed the fundamental evil of the human condition.

If one compares Sōseki's view of human nature and the dangers of individual freedom with most popular early Meiji works like Tokutomi Roka's *Hototogisu* (Namiko, 1900) or Ozaki Koyo's *Konjiki yasha* (Gold Demon, 1897–1902) which viewed human unhappiness as the result of restrictions imposed by the old social system, one can clearly see the development that had occurred in Japanese thought since the beginning of modernisation. This process, also familiar in Europe, represents a transition from the externalisation to the internalisation of evil whose source is ultimately found in human nature. The changes that took place in the I-novel from Tayama Katai to Dazai Osamu follow a pattern of similar development. One can therefore attempt a statement that Japanese literature, like its Western counterpart, reveals ideas closely associated with the process of modernisation which begins by fighting the restrictive social order only to find that the final battle has to be fought within the individual himself.

Sōseki himself never found a satisfactory solution to the problem that constituted the main theme of his later works and at the end of his life he withdrew from the battle into the world of religious contemplation. He thought to find harmony by viewing human life as visited on one by Providence and attempted to reconcile himself to circumstances through a kind of self-abandonment which was practised in the Buddhist religion. To abandon one's worldly desires, to relinquish one's selfish nature, to de-emphasise and suppress to a certain extent one's own individuality in order to bring a more harmonious relationship with others: this was the essence of the religious position that Sōseki adopted in his final attempt to overcome what he perceived as the fundamental ugliness of human nature.

Thus in the case of both Mori Ōgai and Natsume Sōseki, the two giants of Meiji intellectual life, the initial search for rationality and harmony led to final positions of withdrawal and resignation. Both positions were rooted in traditional oriental thought which offered the idea of *jiko hōki*, the abandonment of self, as a solution to human problems, and which perceived social life in terms of isolated individuals whose existence did not threaten the lives of others.

Itō Sei perceives a similarity between the final stand of Sōseki and Ōgai, and the attitude of the *bundan* writers who abandoned society. Ōgai and Sōseki lived in society and wrote novels in which they developed their logical and analytical view of the world; their works are read and loved by the nation. But in the end they adopted the posture of self-abandonment, which suggests that, like the *bundan* writers, they saw no scope for the development of their ideas within Japanese society.[20] The fact that they did not follow the *bundan* writers in abandoning society but resorted to inner withdrawal, taking up the stance of passive observers, was mainly due to their strong links with society, which had come about, in Ōgai's case, through privileged social status, and in Sōseki's case, through fame as an established writer.[21]

SHIRAKABA AND SHIGA NAOYA

Shirakaba was a group of young and idealistic writers who inherited the rational spirit of Natsume Sōseki and Mori Ōgai. They took the name from the magazine they started publishing in 1910. Quite unknown at the time, they all acquired undisputed rank as writers within a few years, and rose to positions of great influence in the *bundan* of the second half of the Taishō period.

All the members of the group, which included Shiga Naoya, the three Arishima brothers, Mushanokōji Saneatsu, Nagayo Yoshio and others, came from the upper classes of Meiji society. Their fathers were aristocrats and former top class *samurai* who had become industrial managers – an environment most favourable to the rational Western ways of thinking. They all grew up in wealth and luxury, and also graduated from the same upper-class high school, Gakushūin, which in Japanese conditions always was a strong unifying factor. It is argued that they were 'more of a school because of their common social background than because of the intellectual and emotional attitudes they shared'.[22]

The world they lived in was very small, and it was limited to the family circle, relatives and friends, but it was the only world where the 'European spirit' based in rational relationships between individuals could prevail.[23] Within the premises of their small world the Shirakaba members were able to bring the rational ideas of Sōseki (who never put them into practice) off the theoretical plane and utilise them in everyday life. They came to maturity while fighting their fathers' incomprehension, while engaging in continuous intellectual battle and mutual criticism with friends, and while searching for a conscientious approach to life. Within their tolerant environment they could safely harbour radical thoughts, criticising the old order of social values and hoping to create new social values that seemed convincing to them as a result of their own experience. They believed that the positive and logical approach to life could solve most problems between parents, friends and lovers. Their faith in the strength of man's rational behaviour, the spiritual inheritance from Sōseki and Ōgai, stood them in opposition to the gloomy world of the naturalists.

While the naturalists, mainly as a result of their country origin, suffered real hardship in life and had a very dark view of society, the Shirakaba members' élitist background made them unafraid of society and its sanctions. While the naturalists went through the emotional trauma of a break with family traditions, the Shirakaba writers, of a younger generation, were emotionally less committed to traditional values and therefore more critical of the irrational aspects of Japanese society. Where the naturalists considered man more in terms of his baseness, weakness and fear of society, the Shirakaba shared a positive approach to the real world and tended to affirm humanity itself. This can be attributed partly to their upbringing but also possibly to the influence of the Christian thought to which they had been exposed in their youth. They saw themselves as men of the world, confident in their moral and aesthetic judgments and their art as a means of spreading their positive views through society. They actually broadened the aesthetic aspects of artistic perceptibility by paying attention to the beauty of painting, pottery and traditional crafts.

Shirakaba rose to a position of unquestioned supremacy in the *bundan* in the mid-Taishō period, gathering under its banner various groups of anti-naturalistic orientation. They injected their own self-confidence and conceit into the pessimistic world of social escapists. The élitist consciousness of the artist and the sense of artistic mission that became the characteristic features of the *bundan* ideology can be traced to Shirakaba's influence. Its members believed that their goals represented the goals of human kind in its progress towards happiness and harmony. The ideal embraced by Shirakabaha was of a morally superior, independent artist who by realising those goals in his life was working for the benefit of man as its pioneer and teacher.

Their belief in the value of their personal experience as artists gave rise to a particular type of *bundan* novel pioneered by Mushanokōji Saneatsu. This was the so-called *jiko shōsetsu*, a personal novel which concentrated on the writer himself and described his relationships with friends and relatives and his love affairs. Also due to Shirakaba's influence was the appearance in the *bundan* of a type of novel referred to as *bundan kōyūroku shōsetsu* – a chronicle of *bundan* friendships, describing the relationships, talks, meetings, and arguments held between writers. This became very popular during the 1920s and it drew the *bundan*'s attention to the psychological inlay of the artist. If the confessions of the naturalistic I-novelist aimed at exposing the weaknesses of human nature, the confessional *jiko shōsetsu* or *bundan kōyūroku shōsetsu* were rooted in the élitist consciousness of the Shirakabaha who believed that, precisely because they were artists, their positive confessions should be of special interest and value to the readers. When in the 1920s the hero of the I-novel became a professional writer combining curiously the mentality of the fugitive slave with self-conceit as an artist, this was attributable to the influence of Shirakaba.[24]

Many of Shirakaba's works, particularly at the early stage, had the I-novel form, but they never, in Itō Sei's opinion, 'practised it in the prelogical naturalistic way'. Itō Sei states that Shiga Naoya's works, in spite of their autobiographical tendency, remind one rather of Ōgai in their clarity of vocabulary and thought. The self Shiga describes is the self of a fighting man, who struggles to bring rational order to the world around him. On principle Shiga does not analyse the self as his exclusive subject; he describes it only in its active relation to the environment. His description of the confrontation between the individual ego and environment has no equal in modern Japan.[25] One might perhaps argue that the construction of the hero in Shiga's works is as in most I-novels, rather less than complete, but there is no doubt that his presentation of an individual as a separate entity working in the environment expressed a new potentiality that had appeared in the lives of modern Japanese and became one source of the undiminishing popularity of his works to this day.[26]

Unlike the I-novelists who sacrificed their lives for the sake of their art, Shiga Naoya stood firmly for preserving harmony in his own life. He used his art as a medium through which he told his readers about the harmonious solutions that he had found to the critical situations in his life. It is generally accepted that in comparison with the I-novelists, who did not have real position in the world and could thus easily abandon their social links in order to write, writers like Shiga Naoya, Shimazaki Tōson, Natsume Sōseki or Mori Ōgai had social positions which they could not easily sacrifice. Their major problem was that of accommodating their art harmoniously to the boundaries of their social lives. Shiga in the most creative period of his life managed to achieve a sense of harmony as an artist and as a living person by reverting to the traditionally oriental concepts of nature, impermanence and death.

The process that transformed Shiga from a modern youth fighting with his social environment for the sake of his individual freedom into a mature man seeking harmony rather than confrontation and nurturing critical doubts about the quality of modern individualism is masterfully described in the only long novel which he ever wrote, *An'ya kōro* (A Dark Night's Passing, 1921–37).[27] The protagonist, thrust into despair by the agonising truth about his birth (he is the child of an affair his mother was having with his grandfather), and later by his wife's infidelity, recaptures the significance of life and a sense of harmony with the world by viewing himself as a part of the natural world. The sense of harmony he arrives at is based on the oriental concept of Nature, of which man constitutes an integral part. Only by seeking unity with the natural world and subjecting oneself to its laws can one achieve a perspective which will enable one to combat the problems of one's life and gain peace of mind.

Shiga's case makes one realise that whenever a danger threatened, even the writers who consciously desired to relate themselves rationally to the world, found stability through the traditional Japanese thought pattern where harmony is conceived in the awareness of the impermanence of all things, and where the awareness of others in society plays no part. Nowhere is it more clearly manifested than in Shiga's masterpiece *Kinosaki nite* (In

Kinosaki, 1917), a work of outstanding beauty which is considered to be a perfect example of *shinkyō shōsetsu*, novels about one's state of mind.

Although it is based on the writer's personal experience, the *shinkyō* novel differs substantially from the naturalistic I-novel. It usually describes in retrospect an event in the author's life which through a perspective of years acquires a significance as a critical test of life from which the author has re-emerged a morally stronger and more harmonious personality. This is how Hirano Ken formulated the essential difference:

> If the I-novel is literature of destruction, the *shinkyō* novel is literature of salvation. If the I-novel is a confession of a critical situation and hopeless confusion, the *shinkyō* novel is the result of being able to control the crisis and find a way out of it. If the former is rooted in the feeling of discord between the self and the world, the latter is groping for harmony; on the one hand there is a consciousness of crisis in life which springs from a sense of hopelessness and a despair at the sinfulness of human existence, and on the other a lucid view of life which has come about as a result of overcoming the crisis. The former seeks salvation in art, the latter in real life. The origin of the former lies in naturalism which offers no ideals or solutions, and the origin of the latter is in the idealism of Shirakaba-ha. In other words, the I-novel is the literature of *hametsugata* and *gensei hōkisha* (the self-destructive and world-abandoning types), while the *shinkyō* novel is the literature of *chōwa mono* and *gensei enjisha* (the harmonious and worldly type).[28]

The following excerpts from *Kinosaki nite* illustrate the concept of harmony expressed in the *shinkyō* novel. The author, recovering from a nearly fatal accident at the spa of Kinosaki, observes three incidents of death which make him wonder about the nature of life and death. The first one concerns a bee:

> One morning I saw a dead bee on the roof. Its legs were doubled tight under it, its feelers dropped untidily over its head. The other bees seemed indifferent to it, quite untroubled as they crawled busily around it on their way in and out. The industrious living bees gave so completely a sense of life. The other beside them, rolled over with its legs under it, still in the same spot whenever I

looked at it, morning, noon, night – how completely it gave a sense of death. For three days it lay there. It gave me a feeling of utter quietness. Of loneliness. It was lonely to see the dead body left there on the cold tile in the evening when the rest had gone inside. And at the same time it was tranquil, soothing.

The second one involves a wounded rat thrown into the river:

I did not want to see the end. The sight of the rat, doomed to die and yet puttings its whole strength into the search for an escape, lingered stubbornly in my mind. I felt lonely and unhappy. Here was the truth, I told myself. It was terrible to think that this suffering lay before the quiet I was after. Even if I did feel a certain nearness to that quiet after death, still the struggle on the way was terrible. Beasts that do not know suicide must continue the struggle until it is finally cut short by death. What would I do if what was happening to the rat were happening to me now? Would I not, after all, struggle as the rat was struggling? I could not help remembering how near I was to doing very much that at the time of my accident.

The third incident, describing the death of a lizard in which the author himself was unintentionally involved, ends the novel:

What had I done, I thought. I often enough kill lizards and such, but the thought that I had killed one without intending to filled me with a strange revulsion. I had done it, but from the beginning entirely by chance. For the lizard it was a completely unexpected death. I continued to squat there. I felt as if there were only the lizard and I, as if I had become the lizard and knew its feelings. I was filled with a sadness for the lizard, with a sense of the loneliness of the living creature. Quite by accident I had lived. Quite by accident the lizard had died. I was lonely, and presently I started back toward the inn down the road still visible at my feet. The lights at the outskirts of the town came into view. What had happened to the dead bee? Probably it was carried underground by that rain. And the rat? Swept off to sea, probably, and its body, bloated from the water, would be washing up now with the rubbish on a beach. And I who had not died was walking here. I knew I should be grateful. But the proper feeling of happiness refused to come. To be alive and to be dead were not two opposite extremes. There did not seem to be much difference between them. It was now fairly dark. My sense of sight took in only the distant lights, and the feel of my feet against the ground, cut off from my sight, seemed uncertain in the extreme. Only my head worked on as it would. It led me deeper and deeper into these fancies.

I left after about three weeks. It is more than three years now. I did not get spinal tuberculosis – that much I escaped.[29]

A critical danger threatening the author's life becomes the source of creative inspiration of the *shinkyō* novel. However, it is not the event itself, but the author's thoughts concerning it, his struggle to grasp the meaning of life in the process of recovery from the crisis, that constitute the important theme of this type of novel, which is often described as the oriental novel of ideas. Its view of life belongs to traditional oriental thought, where man is a part of a cosmic reality embracing all living things and accepts his natural fate with a 'god-like passivity'. The inevitable sadness of living permeates that sense of harmony.[30]

There is a clear line of writers in modern Japanese literature who shared the affirmative approach to life. It stretches from Shiga Naoya, through Takii Kōsaku (1894–), Kajii Motojirō (1901– 1932), Hōjō Tamio (1914–1937) to Shimagi Kensaku (1903–1945) and Ozaki Kazuo (1839–). Of their works which express the harmonious ideal, most belong to the *Kinosaki nite* pattern of thought structure. They invariably describe the author's slow ascent from the depth of crisis towards an acceptance of life which is ultimately based on the awareness of *mu* (impermanence) and death. The sense of existence becomes clear only when it is threatened by death. That the threat was real and not imaginary was confirmed by the authors' own lives: Kajii Motojirō died young of tuberculosis, so did Hori Tatsuo and Shimagi Kensaku. Hōjō Tamio's hero in *Inochi shoya* (Life's First Night, 1936) is a leper and the author himself died of the disease in a lepers' hospital. The appeal of these works lies in the expression of hope and will to live, in spite of the potentially destructive crisis that threatened the authors' lives.

The harmonious view of life and the self-destructive view of life, that flow in two main currents through *bundan* literature, occasionally touching and influencing each other, are discussed by Itō Sei and other literary critics in terms of two types of mentality, the so-called ascending (*jōshō ninshiki*) and descending (*kakō ninshiki*) perceptions of life. For both types it is a critical situation in life and, in extreme cases, the threat of death that becomes the source of creative inspiration, but while the ascending type concentrates on the effort of rising from death, the descending type deliberately tempts it. A work like *Kinosaki nite* starts at the zero point, at the very depths of human existence and proceeds in a slow ascent to the surface; in the works of Dazai Osamu and Tanaka Hidemitsu a comprehension of life occurs in the process of dying, falling back from the surface and slowly sinking to oblivion.[31]

The ascending and descending mentality in modern Japanese literature is often viewed in terms of the 'materialistic' argument, favoured by Hirano Ken and Ara Masahito, who emphasise that those writers who came from a privileged and happy environment, turned to idealism and social reform and created the ascending form of art, whereas those with a social inferiority complex turned to the old pattern of self-destruction and created the descending form of art.

Itō Sei, criticising that view as oversimplified, points to the influence of the characteristically *bundan* phenomenon where the I-novelist could not escape his I-novel image in real life and had to some extent to adjust his life to that image: 'This turned the ascending type into moral reformers, politicians and revolutionaries, and led the descending type into the destruction of family, escapism, drugs, and suicide.' In either case, he writes, the *bundan* writers found themselves at the end of the road. Once they established a harmonious relationship with their environment, once the family peace was firmly preserved, they could not, like Shiga Naoya, write novels any more. Harmony in life could not be preserved without a hidden sacrifice on the part of the artist. At the other end of the scale the artist in pursuit of his art destroyed himself, thus bringing his art to its logical conclusion.[32]

The literary works produced by both the ascending and descending types represent what Itō Sei calls the 'vertical' method in Japanese literature. The writers, regardless of whether they are of harmonious or destructive orientation, search for the meaning of life and the sense of human existence through an awareness of death and impermanence. Events are described only in so far as they convey the author's ideas concerning them. Japanese writers of pure literature ignore the 'horizontal' type of description, common in the West, that deals with complicated social relationships, human psychology, laws of human behaviour, etc. Instead they treat most subjects through the predominant 'vertical' method. If one looks for instance at the treatment of love in Japanese literature, one finds at once that it is combined with the notion of death (e.g. *shinjū*, love suicides). We do not, says Itō Sei, move from love horizontally towards the others in society but connect the emotion with death. This is where Japanese writers excel – in the vertical method that leaves no room for social concern.[33]

In the background of the vertical literary method lies a vertical way of thinking which developed in the course of Japanese history. The Eastern philosophies of life contained in Buddhism, Taoism and Confucianism lack the positive precepts of Christianity in relation to social behaviour. Confucianism which was originally concerned with the social system stressed the vertical type of lord–vassal relationship. It also became the backbone of feudal morality by teaching the abandonment of self in the name of loyalty to one's social superior. Thus the Japanese over a long period were subject to the pressures of vertical systems and developed a vertical mentality, which ultimately viewed the human condition in terms of death and the impermanence of things. Marxism and Christianity (which spread widely only after the Second World War) were the two systems of thought which influenced the Japanese in the direction of horizontal thinking.[34]

An example of the active approach to life and the social zeal of the ascending type may be found in the two extra-literary ventures undertaken by Shirakaba members: Mushanokōji Saneatsu's *atarashiki mura* (new village, 1919) and Arishima Takeo's renunciation of his father's inheritance (1922).

The *atarashiki mura* was a movement started by Mushanokōji, who purchased land in Kyushu with the intention of creating there the prototype of an ideal community in which all inhabitants could live like 'brothers'. The plan was realised in 1919. *Atarashiki mura* was a community of people who worked voluntarily, producing only enough to support themselves and devoting the rest of the time to the 'realisation of self'. Mushanokōji himself worked there for eight years. The project has importance in that it was, firstly, an example of a Japanese modern novelist actually translating his social ideas into practice; and secondly, it was an important attempt at constructing an ideal society through a completely idealistic concept, before materialism had taken root in Japan.[35] Mushanokōji conceived a self-righteous, rational society and tried to actualise it in the colony he founded. The experiment failed, however, because according to Itō Sei Mushanokōji's rationality had no validity in Japanese society as it actually existed. It was the rationality of an ego, inflated by the upper-class notion of good, which was determined to create an idealistic society by its own force without recognising the resistance which was coming from the environment.[36]

Arishima took a different course from Mushanokōji and in 1922 divided the land which he had inherited among his tenant farmers, renouncing his own rights to it. In his eyes he was only doing justice to the people working on the farms by declining the unjust profit which as absentee landlord he would be stealing from them. In abandoning his own rights to the estate and giving land to the people who were actually living there, the farmers, Arishima revealed a more profound understanding of social reality than Mushanokōji ever did.

Arishima was not a typical Shirakaba member. He was older than most of the other members and also more conscious of his social responsibility. He had been interested in socialism since his youth, and the fact that his social and financial standing was entirely different from that of the proletariat came to torment him all his life. The more the socialist movement gained ground in Japan, the more his endeavours to square his life with his socialist ideas proved futile. Temporarily he maintained psychological equilibrium by making frequent donations to the socialist movement, but the time came when this ceased to be a solution. Finally he arrived at the conclusion, expressed in *Sengen no hitotsu* (A Declaration, 1922), that the labour movement should be carried on by labour itself, and that he himself, coming from the ruling class, could only 'shut his eyes in resignation'. This consciousness of self-bankruptcy became a strong factor hastening his death. He had an affair with another man's wife and the two lovers committed suicide together. Arishima was then forty-five. Ostracised by society for his love affair, and not being able to bear the scandal, Arishima who praised the joy of love in his works, was defeated and destroyed in his confrontation with Japanese social reality.

Nevertheless Arishima's sense of social responsibility led him further than any other Shirakaba member into the world of social conflict. On the whole the concept of society did not enter the *bundan* literature of the Taishō period; his *Sengen no hitotsu* remained largely outside the sphere of *bundan* interests. The harmony which these writers envisaged was built within the framework of their individual lives and limited to their own particular experiences. They felt that the realisation of self was the most important object of the artist and that social action was justified only within the limits of individual fulfilment and happiness. One can say that the concept of the ego actively organising its environment in a liberal spirit was expressed in Japanese literature for the first time through Shirakaba.[37] It appeared in the interval between the nihilism of the social escapists and the 'pure objectivity' of the passive observers, and it made a vivid impression on the Japanese intellectual world.

Nevertheless, Itō Sei argues that under the circumstances of Taishō Japan the ideal of rational behaviour presented by the Shirakabaha was no less of a literary illusion than the naturalistic ideal of a free man, since it was only possible in one small section of Japanese society. It was this combination of material well-being and unique family and friend relationships that produced in the individual a desire to relate himself rationally to his environment. Shiga Naoya with his iron will was more successful than anyone else in putting his ideas into practice within that world. Yet, when Shiga's ethic, based on his own tastes and moods, came into contact with the outer world, where the notion of the self-asserted individual did not exist, it 'always revealed the bankrupt characteristics which may be defined as the egoism of the privileged classes'. Shiga's art was only possible in the very unusual circumstances of a not yet fully-established bourgeois environment being confronted by a very strong and active personality.[38]

The Shirakaba-dominated *bundan* effectively strengthened its élitist and isolationist image *vis-à-vis* society. This tendency became particularly pronounced towards the end of the Taishō period when the *bundan* found itself under attack from two directions – it was denounced by the proletarian movement for its lack of social involvement and by popular literature for its exclusiveness.

CONCLUSION

In a summary of the discussion of *chōwa*-type attitudes among Japanese writers, the following points should be made:

(1) A logical and harmonious way of thinking attracted writers from well-to-do families and those who had established their positions in society as writers relatively quickly. Their effort to live rationally and at the same time harmoniously has to be appreciated

as a task difficult to achieve within the social and political framework of pre-war Japan. But one should also remember that without the position and the financial means which they possessed and, connected with it, the sense of security, they would have never been able to achieve it. They represented families and positions which did not reach even five per cent of Japanese society.[39]

(2) If their views on social harmony, judged by today's standards, are found rather unsatisfactory it is mainly, in Itō Sei's view, on two accounts: they seemed to be mostly unaware of the deeper subconscious layer of human psychology that often motivates man's behaviour, and also, as a result of their privileged social position, they lacked the social perspective and the insight that would enable them to penetrate the world of social conflict welling up just below the surface. They described some fundamental aspects of human behaviour in such relationships as between man and woman, parents and children, son of a rich family and maid, poor writer and publisher, but very rarely does one find a description of the fear and instability that comes from differences in social and economic position. It surfaces sometimes in the works of Sōseki and Shiga, but it is not something which would deeply disturb their spiritual balance. They describe position and rank as a part of human fate like the ugliness or beauty of one's face.[40]

(3) Despite the above criticism, Itō Sei ends with a positive evaluation of the *chōwa*-type attitudes adopted by those writers. In his opinion, it should not be surprising that the idea of harmony as expressed by them does not seem satisfactory today. Harmony can exist and be valid only under certain circumstances, and when those circumstances change, when new factors appear, the harmony as understood up till then becomes obsolete, in spite of the fact that it has been created with great expenditure of energy, talent and good will. Such is the law of development of human history. But the effort of those who in Japanese conditions created the thought of logical harmony has not been wasted.

(a) Their thought formed a basis on which a sense of harmony that encompassed social class consciousness developed. The example which Itō Sei brings forward is that of Miyamoto Yuriko (1899–1951) in whose life and works the transformation from the Shirakaba type of idealistic humanism to the Marxist type of harmony based on the idea of social justice was quite conspicuous. Miyamoto came from an upper-middle-class family, wealthy enough for her father to send her on a study trip to America. Her perception of society never developed fully, but if at the beginning of her literary career (she started publishing in 1916) she seemed to be convinced that the problems could be resolved by nothing more than righteousness and individual good will, she later developed a sense of harmony that extended to include social classes. She became connected with the Marxist literary movement writing mainly about the social problems of women. She had a strong belief in fundamental human rights and it was her sympathy with the Japanese masses which she saw as deprived of any rights, that made her join the Japanese Communist Party. She kept her ideology unchanged even during the war and did not convert, becoming one of the main literary figures of the post-war period.[41]

(b) The ideal of harmony envisaged by the *chōwa* writers of the Taishō period did not encompass society. It was envisaged in terms of individual effort and personal experience and that is where its limitation lies. It ultimately concentrated on preserving spiritual balance in life within the framework of the oriental concept of harmony, where the individual exercises a degree of self-control over his natural desires in order to achieve a more harmonious relationship with others, and where human life is viewed as subject to the same laws as the whole of the natural world. This view undermines to a certain extent the importance of individual purpose and inclination, by making him aware of the inevitability of his fate. Nevertheless, as the writers reformed their view and retreated in the course of their lives from the Western-inspired ideal of purely rational self-righteous actions performed by a strongly motivated individual towards a more Japanese and harmonious view of life, they created a lasting ideal of harmony that still bolsters the lives of Japanese even today. This explains why these writers are still read, appreciated, imitated and help up as paragons.[42] Their ideas, containing as they do elements of Christianity, Buddhist and Chinese thought, have gradually entered and become an inherent part of the Japanese people's way of thinking. In their search for modern solutions, they did not destroy, but developed and enriched Japanese thought.

5 In Search of Beauty

The writers to be considered in this chapter belonged, alongside the Shirakabaha, to the anti-naturalist camp in the *bundan*. Unlike the Shirakabaha, however, they did not have any real quarrel with the naturalistic view of life as such. What they objected to was the 'artless' technique of the I-novel. They refused to praise a simple description of life as the 'spirit of prose'. They could not accept the naturalistic belief that the essence of art lies in the chronicle of one's personal experience. They believed that a work of art should possess a life of its own, independent from the reality of the artist's life. Thus they stressed the importance of artistic method and structure in the work of literature, and aimed at a mastery of that method that would enable them to create works of perfect beauty, appealing to the imagination and senses of the readers. Stimulating subjects and fascinating imagery, that would be matched by an artistically perfect style, were the ideal they pursued. For that reason they are referred to as 'aestheticists' (*tanbi-ha*) or, in Itō Sei's slightly broader terminology as 'methodologists' (*hōhōsha*).

The methodologists were more concerned with structural form and the beauty of artistic expression than their own way of life. In the Taishō period there were Tanizaki Jun'ichirō, Satō Haruo, Nagai Kafū, and Akutagawa Ryūnosuke, and they were followed in the Shōwa period by Yokomitsu Riichi, Kawabata Yasunari, and others. Their activities concentrated round the three coterie magazines that appeared at the end of the Meiji and continued into the Taishō period: *Subaru*, *Mita bungaku* and *Shinshicho*. They also had their own literary club in the down-town area of Tokyo called 'Pan-no Kai' (Pan Society), where most of them met. Bored with the uncompromising stance and the narrow scope of the I-novel, they tried to depict the reality of modern Japan in a logically and aesthetically satisfying manner. They hoped that this new artistic method would enable them to express the consciousness of modern man objectively as was done by modern European writers. At the same time it had to be a method which would fulfil their requirement of artistic perfection. This double aim made the Taishō aestheticists seek inspiration in two considerably different literary models, the writings of Mori Ōgai and Izumi Kyōka (1873–1939).

Mori Ōgai (who with the novelist Ueda Bin was the co-founder of the magazine *Subaru*) was a natural precursor of the Japanese methodologists. He represented the European method, which operated by the application of logic to the subject of description. The material was organised in a structural way, and a logical analysis of the hero's thoughts and actions was aimed at. By this method the writer's personal views appeared only in a disguised and conceptualised form. Ōgai's efforts contributed to the establishment of an independent base for imaginative literature in Japan.

Although the *bundan* aestheticists inherited Ōgai's interest in the literary 'method', their views on art were diametrically opposed to those of Ōgai and other writers of rational and harmonious orientation who envisaged the role of art to be one of active engagement in the cause of the progress of human kind. The aestheticists were dedicated to the idea of the supremacy of art, which was close to the European concept of 'art for art's sake'. They were strongly influenced by the views of Oscar Wilde who emphasised the aesthetic and non-utilitarian aspects of art. Here beauty of form and the artist's skill mattered more than content. The 'art-for-art's-sake' artists believed that art should transcend the reality of life and nature – in their search for perfect beauty they withdrew from realism and explored the world of fantasy. They also believed that a work of art should be judged by aesthetic criteria alone – there was no room for moral considerations as art transcended morality. In fact, most of them discovered or came near to discovering that beauty was often an accomplice of evil and the artist a devil's disciple, as his tireless pursuit of artistic perfection could cause him to forget the principles of common humanity.

All these elements can be traced in the works of the Japanese aestheticists. At the same time, the Japanese ideal of the 'supremacy of art' acquired characteristic features of its own due to the circumstances under which it evolved in Meiji Japan. For example, it emphasised the idea that the establishment and development of the individual could be accomplished through art, reflecting thus the general confidence of Meiji Japanese in individual freedom and personal achievement as the means of advancement in life (a

phenomenon referred to in Japanese by the term *risshin shusse*). The
Meiji idea of art as the ultimate and self-redeeming purpose of the
artist's life acquired, however, a special meaning through its
association with traditional reclusive and self-destructive thought.
Traditionally, the popular image of an artist in medieval times was
that of a hero who chose isolation so that he might develop some skill
or technique through rigid self-discipline and ascetic practices, and
subsequently became a peerless master. Many hermits, swordsmen
and famous artisans, who had become what they were by isolating
themselves from society, were in fact social rebels. Eccentrics and
isolationists, these men cared for nothing but their own art, the
almost mystical mastery of which became the basis of their identity.
They entered society only temporarily through their art and talent.
Meiji literature perpetuated that image. A newly-acquired confidence in the importance of literary art made the writers create
heroes who advanced to a position of social success by mastering
some art, and they thereby inspired the young Japanese of the time
to attempt the same.[1]

The belief in the redeeming qualities of art is very strongly
expressed in the works of Kōda Rohan (1867–1947). The protagonists of his three novels, written between 1889 and 1891, *Furyū Butsu*
(Elegant Buddha), *Ikkoken* (A Sword) and *Gojū no tō* (Pagoda) were
respectively a sculptor, swordsmith and carpenter, who through
their diligent and single-minded application produced perfect
works of art and consequently gained fame and success. However,
their application was not socially motivated. It aimed at self-
fulfilment and individual happiness conceived outside the framework of society. Indeed, only by ignoring society and its restrictions
could they devote themselves completely to their art. Rohan's works
conveyed to Meiji readers and critics alike the sense of inner
discipline and purity of pursuit that he believed were the attributes
of the artistic profession. The Meiji idea of individual effort being
the means to social success, which the writers along with everybody
else shared at the time, is supplanted in Kōda Rohan's novels by a
more traditional image of an artist as a social recluse with a passive
attitude to the outside world, hoping to reach society only through
the rigour of his art.[2]

Art as the only redeeming factor in the artist's life emerges very
clearly in the works of Izumi Kyōka (1873–1939). His novel *Uta
andon* (A Song and a Lantern, 1911),[3] which achieved tremendous
popularity in his stage and later film adaptations, tells the story of a

young and talented No^- artist whose skill and devotion to his art protect him during the greatest crisis of his life.

In Itō Sei's view, Izumi Kyōka was the first practitioner of the new aesthetic method in modern Japanese literature.[4] He came from the *Ken'yūsha* school, where he was one of Ozaki Kōyō's favourite pupils, and after Kōyō's death, when most of his contemporaries degenerated into popular novelists or joined the naturalist movement, he remained independent. Kyōka's works established new standards of artistic prose. He was fascinated by the past and drew his material from old tales of mystery, from the *Kabuki* theatre and from classical Chinese literature. Yet he expressed this spirit of the past in the modern Japanese language (*Kōgo*), in a compact, rapid style filled with fanciful images of the sort used until then only in poetry. He achieved in his works a crystallisation of sensual beauty. His grasp of sensuality, however, was not of the old, *gesaku* type; it did not depend on the inherent sensuality of the subject, as was the case with the writers of the Edo period. It was brought to life in the atmosphere and literary style of his works by his new technique of expression.

Mori Ōgai and Izumi Kyōka, in contrasting ways, introduced into modern Japanese literature a deliberate concept of method through a rationalisation of thought and structure. Those two types of artistic effort represented two basic models which, combined in various degrees, formed the foundations for the literature of the Japanese aesthetic school.

However, in developing the new artistic method further, the aesthetic writers proceeded clearly in the direction indicated by Izumi Kyōka rather than Mori Ōgai. The major Taishō period writers of the aesthetic school, Tanizaki Jun'ichirō, Satō Haruo, Murō Saisei and Satomi Ton, were all influenced by Kyōka's style. Even the writers of the Neo-sensualist School, Shinkankakuha,[5] such as Kawabata Yasunari and Yokomitsu Riichi who in the early years of Shōwa looked for modern means of expression in prose, were later drawn towards Kyōka's method and ended, like Kyōka, in the pursuit of purely sensual effects.[6]

The emphasis on the sensual aspect of beauty indicates, in Itō Sei's view, the strength of the traditional concept of beauty latent in modern Japanese literature. In Japan, traditional arts such as No^- drama, puppet *Jōruri* theatre and the *Kabuki* theatre developed an idea of beauty which was abstracted from the reality of feudal society. Due to the nature of feudal society, which suppressed logic in favour of obedience by controlling and formalising all aspects of human life, an ideal of beauty evolved that concentrated on sensuality as the only aspect of life that flourished relatively unrestrained. The pursuit of sensual effects was inherited through Izumi Kyōka by the modern Japanese methodologists.[7]

Closely linked to the sensual aspect of beauty was the special character of the language employed by the aestheticists to convey that sense of beauty. The class distinctions of feudal society persisted in the language of the arts in Japan. Such distinctions were difficult to transcend as they were expressed partly by differences in the use of words themselves. There was no fluidity of usage between social classes. Hence the feudal stratification of the arts tended to remain unchanged. The use of artistic language in Japan stands in direct opposition to the way language was used in Europe. There language appeared as a means of conveying logical processes of thought, and was easily understood by all classes. The works which are valued in the European tradition are complex psychologically not linguistically; they belong to the realm of logic not to that of the senses. In Japan language was employed illogically for a mainly decorative effect, and the words were used in such a way that they acted as elements of sensual beauty. Consequently, the works which sought highly artistic modes of expression irrevocably moved away from the reality of life. The writers who aspired to purity and perfection in artistic expression were inevitably led, like Izumi Kyōka, towards traditional sensuality.[8]

The origin of the paradoxical situation in which the 'method-ologists' found themselves – their 'tragedy' as Itō Sei prefers to term it – lies here. The more they mastered the method of artistic expression, the more they turned away from reality, losing in that way the only environment where the rational occidental approach could operate. Most of those who started out by adopting the Western method, at some point fell into this trap as a result of striving for the intense effect of which the Japanese style was capable. However much they wanted to portray scenes from modern Japan in the way Western writers portrayed their societies, they had to face the fact that the Japanese order of beauty was essentially isolated from real society. They were bound to be conscious that their artistic method would collapse and their order of beauty would tumble if it came into contact with the vulgar reality of life.[9]

This limited severely the scope of their works. It affected the choice of subject, which had to accord with their sense of beauty. They were forced by the requirements of their methodology to choose subjects appropriate to a life of leisure. Exoticism, a romantic view of the past and the exploitation of Chinese and European materials were the popular choice among the aestheticists. In this order the writer may appear as a subject, but he can only be described as a character out of touch with reality, a type of social recluse engaged in the pursuit of an ideal of artistic perfection.[10]

Compared with the *bundan* methodologists, the I-novelists possessed at least a real human environment. Their families, friends, their love affairs, their misery, publicity, or the business of selling their literature provided models from which they could draw material and against which they could test their method. The aestheticists either had to concentrate on a sensual aspect of life, or they had to draw their material from the worlds of medieval and foreign fantasy.

Itō Sei considers that there have been many writers of this type in modern Japan. Their consciousness was modern, but as their work matured they naturally became alienated from reality. Only those who abandoned their yearning for modernity have been able to proceed to artistic perfection. Examples of this are Tanizaki Jun'ichirō, Murō Saisei and Kawabata Yasunari. It is the sad fate of the Japanese methodologist that once he becomes a pursuer of beauty he has to abandon the rational approach to reality.[11]

TANIZAKI JUN'ICHIRŌ (1886–1965)

This was the choice instinctively made by Tanizaki Jun'ichirō, who created in his works an order of beauty which existed without making any concessions to the logic of reality. The novelty of his works comes from the 'logic of the senses' that he established in its place. He created a system built on personalities of tangible sensuality, men whose lives were directed by instinct and the senses. Tanizaki's knowledge of modern psychology, particularly the psychology of sex, gave a new depth to this approach. Tanizaki portrayed in his works the weakness of man driven by sexual impulses. He described sex not as an ethical problem, but as man's strongest incentive in life. His famous works like *Chijin no ai* (Fool's Love, 1924–5) or *Manji* (A Tangled Relationship, 1928–30) portray the terrifying results of man's sexual drive, which can bring destruction to family, morality, and even life. They give expression to the growing anxiety of modern man as he realises that the danger which threatens him, comes from his own nature. In comparison with the I-novel, which recorded only the surface experiences of one's private life, this was obviously a new method. If there had been no Tanizaki Jun'ichirō, there would be a gap in modern Japanese literature's endeavours to portray the ego of modern man.[12]

The sensual method refused to accept into its order what lay outside the grasp of the senses and this had an important effect on the writers themselves. In Itō Sei's opinion the 'egos' of the aestheticists took on the aspect of totally devoted servants of their method, that is servants of sensual beauty. As a result the martyr type who would abandon all for the sake of beauty, became such a common subject that it sometimes seems to monopolise their works.

This is epitomised at a very high level by Tanizaki in *Shunkinshō* (A Story of Shunkin, 1933). This work portrays a young man who derives almost masochistic pleasure from submitting himself completely to a beautiful and blind *koto* player named Shunkin. When Shunkin's face is disfigured as a result of a fire, the man blinds himself in order to preserve the image of her beauty in his mind, thus accomplishing the final act of devotion.

Variation on this subject forms the core of all works of the modern Japanese aesthetic movement, from Izumi Kyōka's *Uta andon* through Akutagawa Ryūnosuke's *Jigoku hen* (Hell Screen, 1918) to Satō Haruo's *Utsukushii machi* (Beautiful Town, 1919) and Kawabata Yasunari's *Kinjū* (Birds and Beasts, 1933).[13]

A severe limitation was placed on the subject matter of the *bundan* aestheticists because it still had to be comprised within the scope of the interests of the *bundan*, which in any case represented an isolated community, thus 'limiting again the limitation' inherent in the method itself: 'A small place, thus doubly fenced in, was the habitat of the explorers of the aesthetic method', writes Itō Sei.

To illustrate the position occupied by the aestheticists within the *bundan*, Itō Sei created an analogy with a monastery, where the monks and hermits practise the teaching of Buddha in the hope of salvation. The methodologists might be compared to those monks who were excluded from the general course of study and were engaged instead in making Buddha's portraits and pictures. Such an occupation, being mainly a matter of technical expertise, was not considered satisfactory by other monks. As a result, while the I-novelists treated outsiders like Mori Ōgai or Natsume Sōseki as writers with academic tastes, they criticised *bundan* aestheticists like Izumi Kyōka, Tanizaki Jun'ichirō, Satō Haruo or Akutagawa Ryūnosuke as writers with bourgeois taste.[14]

One further point that should be mentioned in connection with aesthetic literature is the subtle change that occurred in the image of the artist himself between the time Kōda Rohan wrote *Furyū butsu* and the time Akutagawa Ryūnosuke wrote *Jigoku hen.* The aesthetic writers themselves remained by no means immune to the moral aspect of the single-minded pursuit of beauty and the unconditional devotion of one's life to art. Gradually the original optimism and idealism of Kōda Rohan gave way to the sense of doubt and disenchantment of Akutagawa Ryūnosuke.

The work that revealed that change of mood very clearly was *Shūzenji monogatari* (The Story of Shūzen Temple, 1911), a play by Okamoto Kidō that gained high acclaim at the time and remains popular to this day. The hero, a famous mask maker, in order to create the masterpiece of his life, which is to be the mask of a dying man, coldly observes and sketches the expressions on the face of his dying daughter. We are presented in this play with a portrait of the mentality of an artist who accepts unconditionally the idea of the supremacy of art. He accepts the fact that to fulfil his mission as an artist he has to sacrifice his natural human feelings towards his family. The dramatic appeal of this work comes from the realisation that the life of the artist creates victims in his immediate environment; that a man, to devote himself completely to his task, in whatever sphere of social life, must stop being humane. It voices the doubt whether a man has the right to make others suffer for the sake of an unlimited expansion of his personality. The work that illustrated that doubt in an extreme form was Akutagawa Ryūnosuke's *Jigoku hen.* The most famous artist in the land, Yoshihide, engaged in the painting of a screen portraying a vision of hell, watches his beloved daughter die in flames so that he can accomplish his task:

> In front of that pillar [of fire] Yoshihide stood rooted. Then, wonderful to say, over the wrinkled face of this Yoshihide, who had seemed to suffer on a previous occasion the tortures of hell, over his face the light of an inexpressible ecstasy passed, and forgetful even of his lordship's presence he folded his arms and

stood watching. It was almost as if he did not see his daughter dying in agony. Rather he seemed to delight in the beautiful colour of the flames and the form of a woman in torment.[15]

The change that occurred in the image of the artist between Kōda Rohan and Akutagawa Ryūnosuke reflects, in Itō Sei's view, the change that took place in Japanese society during that period. When the feudal system broke down, artists and scholars alike were filled with hope and optimism. They believed they were now free to explore their talents and develop their personalities. Their number was very small but they exerted great influence.

In the mid-Meiji period the number of intellectuals gradually increased and social competition became a feature of life. It was hampered, however, by the social restrictions such as the master–pupil relationship (in *Gojū no tō* the artist is dismayed to find himself competing against his teacher). The artist had to be aware of the fact that his success might bring harm to his adversary (in *Uta andon* the young man's success causes the death of the man against whom he has competed). This was a process of gradual realisation that the freedom of the individual, on which modern life was based, was not unlimited and posed a threat to others.

With the consolidation of the Imperial State towards the end of the Meiji period, competition grew even stronger and with it the need for even more forceful self-assertion on the part of the individual. The terrifying results of unrestrained expansion of the individual ego which is capable of sacrificing even those who are nearest to it for its own sake, are contemplated in *Jigoku hen*. At the same time the artists were confronted with a state where modernity presented only a superficial layer under which the old ways of thinking and the feudal foundations of Japanese society remained unchanged. They became aware of the fact that they could only fulfil themselves by clashing with the old order, consequently creating victims among those around them. The immediate victim of the artist was his family.[16]

This belief in the artist's right to sacrifice his life and his family for the sake of his art was shared, as has been observed earlier, by the *bundan* I-novelists, who originally aimed at the destruction of the old social order. In this sense both the methodologists and the I-novelists were the exponents of the idea of the supremacy of art. But while this belief was contemplated only theoretically by the art-for-art's-sake writers, the I-novelists 'put it into practice by their own way of life'. When an author like Tayama Katai confessed his love affair, he created a work of art that gained him recognition and established him as an artist, but at the same time he brought suffering to himself, his wife and children. His self-sacrifice, which was made in order to create what he considered true art, is in spirit the same as the one described in *Jigoku hen*.[17]

The difference between the two methods of novel writing that developed in the Japanese *bundan*, the confessional and the artistic, lay therefore not in their approach to art, as art was the sacred and ultimate aim common to both, but in what they thought constituted art. In the case of the I-novelists it was the way of life that became the way of literature, and in the case of the aesthetic movement it was the way of description that mattered most. But the division was by no means always clear, and many writers spent their lives oscillating between one method and the other.[18]

In Itō Sei's view it depended very much on the circumstances of the *bundan* itself, whether the writers felt free to write I-novels, or had to resort to fiction. The restrictions of the Meiji *bundan* and its feudal order, favoured fiction; but when, after the Russo-Japanese war, writers felt suddenly freer, that freedom created favourable conditons for self-confession.[19] The I-novel appeared when conditions were right for a quest for truth and individual conscience, and it declined when the expansion of commercial journalism at the end of Taishō and the beginning of Shōwa sealed its fate. Life in the *bundan* at the time, closely intertwined with the fortunes of the publishing industry, lost its freedom and independence. Its order came to resemble the order of the outside world, and it became as restrictive to the writer as were the institutions of family or company to the average man. It was at this point that the necessity for fiction arose, as a man who belongs to the system cannot write I-novels. Criticism of the *bundan* could only be accomplished through Akutagawa's method.[20]

The affinity between the aesthetic and the naturalistic view of life has been mentioned by many literary critics apart from Itō Sei. Hirano Ken's theory concerning the 'supremacy-of-art' mentality of the Japanese I-novelist has been described in an earlier chapter.[21] Writing about Tanizaki Jun'ichirō in his *Waga sengo bungakushi*, Hirano Ken points out that the same fear of the outside world, the same feeling of the hopelessness and the basic cruelty and brutality of human life, existed beneath Tanizaki's artistic mask as that exposed openly in the I-novel.[22] Nakamura Mitsuo in *Tanizaki*

Jun'ichirō ron emphasised this similarity even more explicitly: 'Naturalism and aestheticism are normally assessed in the history of literature as two opposed concepts. But as with many trends of the same period that oppose each other, these two literatures are like Siamese twins, whose faces are turned in opposite directions but through whose bodies circulates the same blood.'[23] Both Tayama Katai and Tanizaki Jun'ichirō 'cut out as much as possible the intellectual aspect from the actions of their heroes degrading them to a purely sensual existence'.[24] One might say that the aesthetic movement proceeded not so much in confrontation with the naturalistic movement, but as its successor, enlarging the biological view of man and stressing the importance of instinct and sensuality. The general direction in which the movement developed was from aesthetic dilettantism with its emphasis on the exotic and the romantic to the pursuit of sensual pleasure. For this it was often subject to the same criticism as its naturalistic counterpart, that is that it was the literature of dissipation.[25]

Finally, two personalities should be mentioned whose literary talent and individuality opened up new ground for the aesthetic movement. One is Nagai Kafū and the other Akutagawa Ryūnosuke.

NAGAI KAFŪ (1879–1959)

Nagai Kafū occupies a special position among the Japanese aestheticists. His long and independent literary life, permeated with a conscientiously critical attitude towards the reality of modern Japan, puts him on a level with the great individualists of the period, Ōgai and Sōseki.

His works, in which he openly extolled the beauty of the female body and declared love and the 'pleasures of the senses' as the goal of life, were respected and admired by the writers of the aesthetic school. The main themes of his works develop within the old gay quarters of the Edo period inhabited by geisha and artists, or concern the cafés, unlicensed prostitutes and dance-hall girls that represented the new urban manners. But his treatment of these subjects goes far beyond a purely sensual approach. Nakamura Mitsuo writes of Kafū as being exceptional in Japan for possessing a theoretical criterion common to those of the aesthetic novelists of the

West.[26] Where Nakamura Mitsuo speaks about a 'theoretical criterion', Itō Sei similarly expresses an opinion that Kafū's ideas 'belong to the order of logic and criticism'.[27] He suggests that although Kafū was drawn emotionally towards the beauty of the old world, in his writings about the gay quarters there is no hint that he was at all intoxicated with the sentiment of this particular world. His approach was not dictated by the desire to pursue the aesthetic method to the point of perfection, but was a matter of intellectual choice.

After his return from abroad (America and France), where he became acquainted with Western thought and literature, Kafū developed a highly critical view of the Japanese social and political system. Distressed by the reality of modern Japan he retreated into the world of fiction, or as Itō Sei expressed it, he 'concealed himself in writing about the feudal world of entertainment.'[28]

Speculating on the reasons behind Kafū's withdrawal from modern life, Itō Sei wrote: 'Kafū himself gave various explanations. Seeing the carriage that was taking the revolutionaries to their place of execution, he thought that not being in a position to help, it would be more appropriate to confine his role to simply that a *gesaku* writer. Or perhaps he thought that Japanese wives were hypocritical prostitutes and that truth lay rather in the lives of streetwalkers. Or else he realised that, after all, he himself was a type of Japanese who lived happily among the remnants of the feudal past.' [29]

Of the three points made by Itō Sei, the first one referred to a well-known passage in Kafū's *Hanabi* (Fireworks, 1919). Kafū, recently returned from abroad, was suddenly reminded by the *lèse-majesté* affair of 1910 of the impracticality of an intellectual revolt against the State. He realised that he could not defend the case of Kōtoku in the way Zola had fought for Dreyfus. In Japan, he concluded, the business of writers had always been and could still only be connected with love, pleasure, sake and geisha, and not with national politics.

Kafū's attitude towards modernisation was clearly negative. In one of his works he wrote: 'This is not reform, not progress, not construction. Meiji means nothing but destruction. The beauty of the old aspects was destroyed only to be replaced by a confusion of all the bad qualities produced overnight.'[30]

The things he found genuine and beautiful in Tokyo were traditional – remnants of the old Edo culture. His sentiment for the

old and his appreciation of Japanese tradition made him idealise the
Japan of the past.

The strong attraction for him of the world of the gay quarters
sprang partly from the fact that it had preserved its freedom and its
independent character, and had been least affected by the fast
process of modernisation. In Meiji society, which was modernising
itself as quickly as possible and at any cost, it offered Kafū a
convenient place of retreat from the pressures and vulgarity of
everyday life. Disillusioned with the political and social reality of
Meiji Japan, Kafū retreated and found a sanctuary in one corner of
society – in the world of geisha and prostitutes, a world which lived
in its own way, possessed a purity and naivety which comforted his
heart, and offered him the freedom for which he was searching. He
found a perfect environment where he was able to portray, in a
fictionalised way, the basic character of himself as a writer and man
who lived according to his own taste, and at the same time give life
to that part of his self which criticised the reality of contemporary
Japan.

Kafū also saw a certain analogy between the world of prostitution
with its mixture of fleeting pleasures, harsh unending suffering, its
accomplishments, its love, its tricks, and betrayals, and the destiny
of a hack writer. He released his ego into the fortunes of the women
who were the object of his description.[31] In this way he was able to
achieve an unusual harmony between his attitude to life and his
literary method, which is the reason why his works embody an
almost perfect expression of his self.[32]

His escape from reality differs from the intuitive escape of the
bundan writers. His choice was conscious and deliberate. He used the
privileges of the literary man to explore the dangers of sex and
society in order to pursue his unique course. According to Itō Sei he
is an example of a writer who succeeded in achieving freedom by
separating himself from society. There was no danger that his
isolation would lead him into self-destruction, as it sprang from a
strongly-rooted system of logic. His isolation enabled him to take the
position of a detached and cool observer of Japanese society, and it
was this distancing that brought his novels to life.[33]

Kafū despised the *bundan* writers for precisely the lack of distance
and self-criticism which made it impossible for them to see their own
position in society realistically. Their self-indulgence, lack of
responsibility and opportunistic hope for success aroused his anger.

A passage from the entry in his diary for New Year's Eve, 1929 (he would become fifty in 1929), is revealing as far as his attitudes to his fellow writers are concerned:

> I have come to think that the happenings of the world have nothing to do with me and I do not concern myself with them. The pronouncements of scribblers are no different from the whining of mosquitoes, and the rumours that are noised about are but a nuisance to make me wish to cover my ears. All my acquaintances tell me that there is no one more fortunate than I, and I am inclined to agree. The first piece of good fortune, I conclude as I look back over my life, is that I have had no fixed wife. Since I have no wife, I have no children or grandchildren, and I can die at any time with no regrets. Since I have no relations with the knights of the literary world, there is no danger that anyone will erect a wretched bronze statue to me when I am dead. The minute a writer dies these days, the people who have gathered about him put up a bronze statue extolling his name, for the purpose of publicising their own names. I myself consider the knights of the literary market-place the dregs of humanity. I shall not, for the moment, speak of myself. The writers of the world know nothing about the world save the cafes and their own rented rooms. They cannot write a letter, they know nothing of courtesy or propriety, they are unable to distinguish what is in good taste from what is not. They are feeble, vacillating, loose, vain, really the most inferior of men. . . . I have to this day numbered no writers among my friends, and this I must count as my greatest blessing.[34]

Nagai Kafū's long life and determined intellectual posture transformed him almost into a legendary hero of modern Japanese literature, to whom are attributed all the charms and attraction of a perfect social recluse.

AKUTAGAWA RYŪNOSUKE (1892–1927)

When Akutagawa Ryūnosuke committed suicide in 1927 at the age of thirty-five, a newspaper commented that 'the sharp sensitivity of a literary man always feels the agony of his time. The death of Kitamura, the death of Arishima, and now the death of Akutagawa. We see the shadows of their times cast on them.'[35] The Marxist interpretation was less sympathetic. They argued that the chaotic and nightmarish quality of his literary works expressed the dying gasp of bourgeois art and that his death symbolically became its epitaph.[36]

Whichever point of view one takes, there is no doubt that Akutagawa's death acquired a symbolic significance for his contemporaries and also for later generations. In immediate terms it marked an end to Taishō aestheticism, and in more general terms it marked an end to the whole epoch of artistic belief in the idea of self-salvation through art, of art as a supreme value in life through which the essence of truth and beauty can be discovered. It marked symbolically the end of the *bundan* idealism, élitism and isolationism. And although the *bundan* modes of thought still persist in some forms in the present day literary world, the *bundan* itself as a pure self-righteous society of lovers of literature headed towards decline after Akutagawa's death. Under the pressures of a changing reality the role of writer and literature had to be redefined.

The problems which Akutagawa wrote about in his works and which he finally found insoluble existed in the conflict between reality and art, between logic and aesthetics. They represented the major *bundan* problems of the time; and the final failure to create a harmony between them, which impelled Akutagawa towards despair and death, may be considered not only the tragic fate of Akutagawa himself, but of all the *bundan*. Akutagawa's work was a test case, where the *bundan* ideas, one after another, were tested and found inadequate in the face of the reality of modern Japan.

First of all it was in Akutagawa's time that the *bundan* system of thought was attacked from outside by the proletarian movement.[37] In Itō Sei's view Akutagawa succeeded in maintaining a harmonious balance between his own kind of rationality and his aesthetic sensibility until the advent of the Marxist movement. The latter represented a more comprehensive kind of rationality than his own, and at this point, as with the Shirakaba writers, he felt that his equilibrium was being threatened. Though this in itself may not have been responsible for his suicide, it is clear that the threat posed by Marxism brought Akutagawa to the brink of psychological collapse.[38]

Akutagawa appeared in the literary world as a master of the aesthetic method and the elegant style. His short stories reveal a sophisticated sense of beauty. He experimented, more comprehensively than any writer before him, with a variety of forms and styles in his effort to create perfect works of art. He was inherently a writer of the art-for-art's-sake movement, a man who found his reason for living in the autonomy of art. As far as his methodological approach was concerned Akutagawa 'wandered restively between Ōgai's logic and Kyōka's sensuality'.[39] An ardent exponent of aesthetic sensibility he tried to introduce logic and a rational analysis of man into the sensual order at the same time. His efforts left him practically in a void, as on the one hand he aimed at a more substantial grasp of reality than the majority of the *bundan* sensualists but on the other could not hope to be accepted by the I-novelists who recognised neither logic nor aesthetics. For them logical analysis was a hindrance that threatened to ruin their method.

It was difficult for a man with a mind as lucid as Akutagawa's to survive in Japanese society, particularly if he insisted on approaching it rationally and critically. He did not manage, like Kafū, to create for himself a special environment in which his art would thrive. Therefore, as long as he chose his material from old Japanese folklore or Christian exoticism, or in a manner of Ōgai, sought analogies by searching into Japanese history, he remained a successful methodologist achieving and preserving a delicate balance between intellect and beauty.

When, however, he applied his logical method to the modern environment, and he himself as well as his fellow writers became the object of his observations, the method turned against him: 'it was simply a case of self-destruction like a snake devouring its own tail'.[40]

Akutagawa tried to save himself by reverting in the latter part of his life to writing 'stories without stories', that is I-novels and *shinkyō-shōsetu* but the anxiety remained. Analysed by intellect, society no longer contained any intrinsic worth. It was the discovery of the sordidness and insanity in life which made him write a story like *Kappa* in 1927; affected by his own method he finally ended by destroying the meaning of life in his works. At the same time, he became one of the first modern writers to question openly the moral and social value of the supremacy-of-art ideal. He suggested that in the struggle between life and art, art might become a force which destroyed the humanity of the artist (e.g. *Jigoku hen*). The advent of Marxism, which mounted a heavy attack on the élitist image of the artist, finally destroyed his belief in the redeeming qualities of art and in its power to save him. Akutagawa became a tragic figure who had lost the meaning of art in life. He was an artist who did not entertain much hope for man and society, but who also denied himself the consolation of art, and in the end he chose death.

It is the case of Akutagawa which proves finally to Itō Sei that the logical direct analysis of the ego brings destruction to the human being. The ego must either be publicised in a pre-logical naturalistic way, as in the I-novel, or it has to appear in disguise as in the European method. Otherwise, in the words of Edgar Allen Poe, 'the burning paper will burn the pen'.[41]

CONCLUSION

The necessity for a logical method in the modern Japanese novel grew as a reaction firstly against the instinctive attachment to naturalistic situations predominant in *bundan* literature and secondly against the *bundan*'s lack of ability to transcend the spirit of practical experience and abstract ideas from reality.

The methodologists, however, found themselves unable to overcome the conflict, inherent in Japanese culture, between art and reality. The traditional concepts surrounding the image of the artist and the means to artistic creativity, when these became sanctioned also by the modern *bundan* way of life, conditioned them to choose art and discard reality.

The aesthetic movement proceeded from an emphasis on the exotic and romantic towards an espousal of the sensual aspect of art. And as the sensual approach represents a fundamentally subjective view of life – life is approached through the sensibility of an individual – the aestheticists moved away from their original aim of a logical representation of reality towards an impressionistic representation which was more in accord with their order of pure art.

Their lack of an objective approach resembled the individualistic and subjective spirit of the I-novel. It is not surprising that many writers tried their hand at both methods, as below the surface differences lay basically the same *bundan* view of art and life. Thus there was established in modern Japanese literature a general trend away from the objective approach and towards a subjective and impressionistic presentation of life.

In some exceptional cases individuals sensitive to the problems of society and the social responsibility of the artist rose in opposition to the spirit of the *bundan*. But either they were forced, in the manner of Kafū, to find for themselves a suitable environment into which they could transfer their existence, or they had to face like Akutagawa a situation in which a logical and critical method of description offered no more than a desperate and ultimately self-destructive act of resistance against the prevailing atmosphere of the *bundan*.

6 The Revolutionary Ideal

IMPACT

Revolutionary, Marxist or 'proletarian' literature, as it was called in Japan, emerged in the late Taishō and early Shōwa periods and captured a commanding position among contemporary literary schools.

Radical literature had existed in Europe since the time of the French revolution, but it only appeared with any force in Japan at the end of the Taishō period when the second wave of Marxism hit Japan in the wake of the Russian revolution. The first wave, often referred to as 'Meiji socialism', had been introduced to Japan at the end of the last century. It was quickly suppressed before it made any real impression on literary circles. It influenced, however, writers like Kinoshita Naoe, Ishikawa Tokuboku and Arahata Kanson, who are usually considered as precursors of the proletarian literature.

The Taishō proletarian literary movement did not last long and with a few exceptions did not produce works of great literary value. Its first coterie magazine *Tanemaku hito* appeared in 1921, and the movement was effectively suppressed by 1935. In spite of the short duration of the proletarian movement its intellectual impact on the *bundan* was enormous.

The great changes which took place in Japan, as in many other countries, as the unexpected consequence of the First World War, found Japanese literary men completely unprepared to receive them. Embittered and disappointed with social reality, they remained indifferent to it; in their enthusiastic search for individualism they a-socialised the individual. The reality of the Taishō period in Japan challenged the intellectuals' social indifference and was explosively receptive to Marxism. The social unrest at the time – a series of strikes, rice riots, economic depression causing widespread unemployment among labourers, intellectuals and white-collar workers, created an atmosphere of general discontent. The incompetent and corrupt political parties seemed to represent only the interest of the upper class. It looked as though the emerging social pattern confirmed and conformed to Marxist predictions. Marxism proved attractive to the Japanese intellectuals as it offered a coherent and scientific explanation of the social reality.

Marxist ideas lie basically within the European tradition of radical social thinking. Social consciousness was a constant element of European intellectual thought which throughout the centuries created many Utopian visions of society. By contrast, the Japanese, starting with *Hōjōki*, created and developed in the course of their history an idealistic image of the social recluse. Traditionally their view of life was supported by the idea of the impermanence of things and by the concept of man as a part of the natural world, not as a part of society. Nevertheless, says Itō Sei, even the Japanese intellectuals were forced to recognise the existence of social forces and to develop their social consciousness under the sheer pressure of capitalist reality. And to them, unused as they were to any form of social thinking, Marxism offered an ideally abstract and logical form of thought, which they accepted almost in its pure form.[1]

Maruyama Masao stresses the attractiveness of Marxism as a universal theory in the Japanese setting:

> Where the particularistic human relations, such as those found in the family, village community, or various sorts of *batsu* (cliques) play a predominant role in determining the pattern of culture, it is in most cases by a strong commitment to a universalistic creed that a man can walk along the path of individual and autonomous decision-making. With the exception of Christianity in the early Meiji period, only Marxism could exert this kind of moral and intellectual influence on a considerable number of people from various strata in modern Japan. It should be remembered that Marxists in prewar Japan . . . turned their backs almost completely on all traditional and nationalistic symbols.[2]

To some extent Marxism corroborated scientifically the intellectuals' intuitive view of society, as a reality restricting individual freedom, in that it placed emphasis on the individual as a victim of the particular social system. As Arima Tatsuo says: 'the naturalists would have felt relieved by such a prognosis of their plight, for the very society that frightened them and refused to understand their individual longings was diagnosed by the Marxists as the source of all evil'.[3] At the same time it offered the intellectuals a decisive means of breaking with the particularistic ties mentioned above in the quotation from Maruyama Masao, a break more drastic than that of their naturalistic predecessors.

Marxism supplied the intellectual with universal knowledge and truth about society, and a definite indication of the role he was to play in society. It commanded that as they knew what ought to be done, they should act accordingly in the real world, so that they would cure the world's ills.[4] It guaranteed the identity of thought and action, thus offering an intellectual and emotional answer to the dilemma of the Japanese intellectual in trying to preserve the integrity of his conscience.

For many young people at the time, this practical aspect of Marxism had the strongest appeal. Marxism brought faith in the rational worth of man – faith that man can manipulate his social and moral lot. There are very many examples of writers referring to Marxist theory as 'rationalism', 'positivism' or 'logicality'. Itō Sei describes the impact that the positivistic message of Marxism had in his young days:

> Since I started writing prose, the literary world has been fundamentally shaken by Marxism. Its practical ethics (*jissenteki na rinri*), which were intended to change the character of literary art inasmuch as it was purely art, had a terrible strength which was difficult to oppose.[5]

Tayama Katai expressed the anxiety of the *bundan* concerning the strength of the pressure exerted by the new political thought, when as early as 1917 in his *Tōkyō no sanjūnen* (Thirty Years of Tokyo) he wrote: 'We had to think about individualism squashed between authoritarian politics and republican politics.'[6]

Tayama's fears were justified in the sense that the proletarian movement, constantly concerned about its relation to politics, denounced the individualistic, uninvolved literature of its predecessors as bourgeois decadence and bourgeois liberalism. Literature was henceforth divided into progressive and non-progressive with all *bundan* literature automatically assigned to the latter category. The revolutionary thinkers regarded the *bundan* writers as tools of the controlling class, and above all, as out of date. The proletarian magazine *Shinkō bungaku* issued a special number under the title *Kisei bundan hakai* (The Destruction of the Existing Bundan), which became one of the main slogans of proletarian literature. By the early 1920s the expansion of proletarian literature, among whose main objectives was the destruction of the old morality and the old *bundan*-consciousness, had reached such a dimension that the established writers felt compelled to define their attitude towards it. Arishima, although attracted by Marxism, expressed his feeling of social impotence in his famous essay *Sengen hitotsu*: not being a worker himself, he felt he could not become a genuine member of the proletarian movement. Others, like Shiga Naoya, felt they could not accept the practical utilitarian aspect of Marxist literature and its involvement in politics.

The *bundan* mentality could not but reject the didactic and moralistic attitude of an engaged literature. After the proletarian movement subsided under extreme government repression and persecution, the *bundan* emotive and egotistic individualism blossomed again and its writers could express their opinions more openly, freed from the fear of being severely criticised for their reactionary views. This period is usually referred to as the period of *bungei fukkō*, revival of literature. This term, describing the atmosphere of the 1930s, expressed the relief and expectations of *bundan* literature, which had at last started to recover from the pressures of the proletarian arts movement. Masamune Hakuchō spoke at the time of Marxist literary criticism as a direct descendant of the moralistic Confucian idea of *kanzen chōaku*:

Are our loyal critics today trying to force our literature into a position defined by their propaganda writings in terms of an "ism" or an ideology? It is just as though these critics were reading Bakin and being impressed by his ideology of *kanzen chōaku*. It is a pre-Tsubouchi Shōyo attitude.[7]

Bundan writers had abandoned the world and achieved in their own eyes an independent position as pure literary men, who could view society with an absolute objectivity. The naturalistic spirit of objectivity and pure observation was in their eyes the only literary method for discovering the truth about life.

In political literature this almost religious attitude of passive observation and acceptance of society came to an end. Marxist literature also destroyed the image of the isolated artist living for the sake of his art, going through hardships in life in order to achieve mastery in what he considered to be true art. It made purely artistic success look dubious in a world of social inequality.

Thus from its ideological standpoint proletarian literature attacked the foundations of the *bundan* mentality. It introduced to modern Japanese literature the problems of modern capitalistic society and demanded a re-definition of the artist's role in it. From the vague awareness of the naturalists and Shirakaba concerning man and society (expressed in terms like *jinsei, yo no naka, seken*) the emphasis shifted towards class society and class politics, and one's class consciousness. Issues like 'politics and literature' or 'politics and thought' entered permanently into the world of literature. The literary self, brought up in an atmosphere of indifference and contempt towards the authority of the State, and towards society and politics in general, found itself suddenly exposed to a violent storm, in which it had to decide upon its course of action.[8]

The proletarian literary movement was short-lived, but it inflicted deep wounds on the consciousness of the *bundan* which are not completely healed even today. The movement attacked as old-fashioned the method of realism based on self-confession, and criticised as traditional and subservient the ethics of non-involvement. It destroyed the self-confidence of the writers by questioning the ethical value of their standards of life and literature. It shook the belief in the meaning and relevance of pure art, symbolised by the I-novel, to contemporary society.

ISOLATION

Nevertheless, viewed within the context of the writers' relation to society, the proletarian literary movement is regarded by many contemporary Japanese scholars as a representative example of an acute problem of isolation. The proletarian writers were committed to a scientific system supposedly embodying the sole and ultimate truth; and as has been mentioned above, through applying this universal truth to 'every minute detail of society' they were led into a decisive break with particularistic ties. To expose oneself consciously to the radiation of 'dangerous thought' even in the form of joining a small study group devoted to Marxism, was an act of determination of a highly individualistic nature. Beside being under constant threat of arrest and torture by the police these young people were in danger of being disowned by angry parents and rejected by all their relatives.

Maruyama Masao describes vividly how 'thousands of families were plunged into an inexpressibly tragic situation overnight by the arrest of their beloved sons and daughters, while their other relatives had also to endure the cold eyes of those around them'.[9] It was not surprising that parents and even teachers, when confronted with the choice, preferred their sons and pupils to become 'pink' (*momoiro*), which meant self-indulgent in sexual pleasure, rather than 'red' (*aka*), i.e. Marxist or Communist. Being labelled with the latter meant virtual excommunication from one's social environment.

The young Marxist intellectuals embraced ideals which were alien to ordinary Japanese, and they found themselves from the outset in the difficult predicament of facing a hostile government on the one hand, and on the other of addressing people to whom purely Marxist symbols meant little. The position of the writers was even more difficult. Their task, writes Arima Tatsuo, was to translate the academic jargon of Marxism into popular symbols. They stood between the Party and the ignorant people. Preoccupied with the necessity for theoretical impeccability as a prerequisite of a conscious proletarian artist, they subjected themselves to the strict political discipline imposed on them by the Party and steadily isolated themselves from the common strata of Japanese society. 'All these writers tried to find their place in society. But their impatient desire to participate was paradoxically to result in their total isolation in the end.'[10]

The difficulties of the proletarian movement are reflected in the literature which they produced. Naturally, in accordance with their beliefs, the young Marxists concentrated their efforts on describing the life of the proletariat and the class struggle. Works describing workers' lives and the labour movement, like Kobayashi Takiji's *Kani kōsen* (The Cannery Boat, 1929), Hayama Yoshiki's *Umi ni ikiru hitobito* (The Sea People, 1926) or Tokunaga Sunao's *Taiyō no nai machi* (The Street with No Sun, 1929) represent that effort, which had the effect of broadening the social perspective of modern Japanese literature.

A large portion of proletarian literature, however, is represented by a type of work which closely resembles the I-novel. This reflected the psychological frame of mind and the mental strain and the suffering of the members of the Japanese intelligentsia who joined the revolutionary movement. Nakano Shigeharu's *Uta no wakare* (Farewell with a Song, 1939) and Kobayashi Takiji's *Tōseikatsusha* (The Life of a Party Member, 1933) belong to this category. In these works there was little substantial criticism of society along Marxist lines. Instead they presented portraits of individuals, often impulsive men who stood up against the oppressive force and determined to fight it with desperate courage on their own; portraits of revolutionary heroes which were based on the personal experiences of the author as a member of the revolutionary movement. In a sense these works can be considered as a revolutionary counterpart of the *bundan* I-novel. In the case of the proletarian writers, however, their starting point was not an escape from society but active opposition to it.

ITŌ SEI'S THEORY OF PROLETARIAN LITERATURE

As we have seen, Itō Sei started his literary career at the beginning of the Shōwa period, when proletarian literature was exerting its strongest influence over the literary world. He was part of the literary movement which defended the autonomy of the artist against the domination of politics over literature. He was the main writer of the so-called New Psychological Literature (*shinshinrishugi bungaku*), which was particularly interested in introducing the new literary method of 'stream of consciousness' from the West. Thus his observations and criticism of Marxist literature are carried out from enemy positions. Nevertheless, they offer one of the most original and incisive interpretations of that movement.

Proletarian writers, he argues, in spite of their fierce attacks on the *bundan*, used the same literary method as the *bundan* writers; and as the literary method, in his view, is a correlation of the writer's mode of thought, the attitudes of proletarian writers towards life could not be much different from those of the *bundan* writers:

I discovered that in its essential character Japanese Marxist literature consisted of information about habits and practices of life and thus had the same character as the I-novel. It continued to supply information about "how we live", and there I saw the *bundan*.

He continues further:

> In theory Japanese Marxists had a broader consciousness of reality, but in fact they stoically practised an idealism which had no dynamism to move within the Japanese reality. They were not simply fugitive slaves, they were fugitive slaves who embraced a desperate conspiracy–therefore removed even further from reality. Like the I-novelists they had a stoical way of thinking and the consciousness of fighting reality, while in fact they were isolated from it. It seems that the relatively easy conversion of literary men was the result of that sense of isolation. And it also was the reason why the form of fictional narrative did not develop in Marxist literature.[11]

The Marxist writers revealed the same 'pure' attitude towards life and literature as was evident in the *bundan*. The *bundan* I-novelist and the Marxist writer shared the same experimental approach to life that made them abandon the world and sacrifice their lives for the sake of their ideals. The important question was not 'how to write' but 'how to live', and the essence of art lay not in the sphere of artistic expression but in a truthful account of the life practices of the hero who embraced an ideal alien to common people. As in the *bundan*, literature became a means of self-assertion through supplying information about the life-style of the isolated hero. Thus, in Itō Sei's view, the Marxist writers contradicted themselves by their method of writing–they were aware of the problems of society but they stood on a limited political platform and used a narrow autobiographical form, which did not express the reality of Japanese society.

A similar view is expressed by the literary critic Hirano Ken. In his essay on Kobayashi Takiji, perhaps the most brilliant proletarian writer, murdered in prison by the police in 1933, he writes that Kobayashi's works, although certainly not intended as I-novels, are 'tinged with the I-novel spirit'.[12] Kobayashi's works *Dokubō* (The Cell), *Hahatachi* (Mothers) and *Tōseikatsusha* (The Life of a Party Member), each respectively reflect in the I-novel way epochs in Kobayashi's life: imprisonment, release from prison, entering the Party, and a life of illegality burdened by the necessity of carrying out clandestine activities as a Party member. The object of description remains the same as in the I-novel: to express the writer's self, the fears and anxieties of a life led completely outside the social system and devoted to a single and unmistakable cause. It is a portrait of an ideal hero, a rebel not broken by the adversities of life.

Even today I have the image of Kobayashi Takiji's *Tōseikatsusha* and Kamura Isota's *Tojō* (On the Road) as works of entirely the same character. I feel like putting an equals sign between the life of Takiji who died a martyr to the cause of the Party and the life of Kamura who died a martyr to the cause of pure literature . . . .

In each case, whether it was a concept of the Party or a concept of pure literature, it represented a symbol of purity, and it was the symbol that mattered most. In the relationship between pure literature and the I-novel, and between the Party and the proletarian novel there was the same ideal of purity and the same total rejection of the mundane [way of life].[13]

What Hirano Ken observed in the passage above was the fact that two diametrically opposed writers of the early Shōwa period – the *bundan* realist Kamura Isota and the proletarian novelist Kobayashi Takiji – reveal the same propensity towards an artistic method which was rooted in the spirit of self-abandonment and which in fact had already begun to decline in their time. They saw self-abandonment as the only way in which they could prove the sincerity of their motives. The motives were naturally different – in the case of Kamura Isota it was the desire to uphold the idea of purity of art, and in Kobayashi Takiji's case it was the desire to fight the unjust social system. The divergence of aims contributed to the conspicuous difference in their works – the former observed and described the abandoned self with a merciless and self-destructive realism to satisfy his criteria of art, while the latter tended to idealise the self in order to satisfy the ideological demands of the Party.

Similarly to Hirano Ken, Itō Sei also suggests that behind the impulse that drove the Marxist writers along the road of political experience lay the Japanese passion for self-abandonment.[14] It was traditionally the only pattern of behaviour which enabled an individual to preserve his integrity and his freedom of thought and action in Japanese society. The attitude of self-abandonment lay at the foundations of the modes of thought and behaviour of the *bundan* writers, and the Marxist writers formed no exception to what seemed to be the general rule that those who want to assert themselves in a society like that of Japan had to abandon that society. A strong individual in the Japanese context is a man whose horizontal links with other members in society are very weak, and who views his existence mainly in relation to the impermanence of the Universe, the oriental concept of *mu*, which traditionally supported the attitude of abandonment.

Marxist writers did not succeed in overcoming this image, as their relation to society was also that of isolation, in spite of their theories of active participation. Itō Sei emphasises the fact that their rebellion was not organised within society, but was an act of desperate revolt executed from outside. Like the conscious withdrawal from the world of the *bundan* writers, the rebellion of the Marxist writers showed the desperation of those who natured the ideals of righteousness and freedom in Japanese society. There is no tradition of revolutionary theory in Japan; there is no tradition of conflict as such in Japanese society, which is based on the principle of harmony (*chōwa*) in social relations.[15] But when the situation becomes unbearable, a desperate, self-destructive rebellion takes place. Japanese history provides ample examples of such desperate acts of rebellion, for example, peasant revolts in the Tokugawa period, terrorist plots in the modern period, and love suicides.

During the Shōwa period the absolutist system which had been established during Meiji reached its climax, and the suppression of thought reached a stage unknown to Western societies. The activities of young idealists, who embraced socialist thought, which for them became the embodiment of truth, logic and justice, were considered illegal in spite of the mainly theoretical character of their involvement. They were persecuted by the government, put into prison and exposed to torture. The suppression pushed them into conversion and withdrawal or into desperate rebellion evoked by hatred for their oppressors where death was no stopping factor. This form of desperate self-destruction is no different, writes Itō Sei, from the self-destruction which the *bundan* writers brought upon themselves through their histrionic flight from society. They are both polar extremes of the same instinct towards the self-destruction inherent in the Buddhist tradition which equates death with the notion of purity.[16]

Within this general trend of the proletarian I-novel, only Miyamoto Yuriko, who had been a follower of the Shirakaba school, took a different attitude. When compared with the numerous revolutionary I-novelists, whose works revealed the tendency toward self-destruction or desperate rebellion, Miyamoto Yuriko's ideas in works like *Banshū heiya* (The Banshu Plain, 1946) or *Dōhyō* (Signpost, 1947) were harmonious and constructive.

Itō Sei's view of the brotherhood of spirit between the *bundan* and the proletarian writer seems to find corroboration in the comment made on Dazai Osamu by the psychologist Minami Hiroshi:

> To Dazai, therefore, his one time participation in the leftist movement was a result of a fellow feeling for 'illegitimacy . . . the man in the shadows . . . criminal consciousness . . . the fugitive from justice' and his response to the disposition of the movement rather than its primary aim. He sensed that as long as he submerged himself in the world of illegitimacy, in which everyone was subject to unhappiness and misfortune, he would not have to suffer among the people in legitimate society.[17]

Dazai's left-wing activity was short lived. His fundamentally pessimistic view of life made him unable to respond to the idealistic Marxist vision of society. Also, the burden of the discipline of an illegal movement, combined with the pressures exerted by the police and his family made him withdraw from active participation. But he clearly considered it one of the major failures of his life, and it contributed greatly to his despair and feeling of inadequacy. Dazai's case seems to suggest that the *bundan* writers, who were drawn into the proletarian movement, may have responded partly to its negative aspects. They felt an affinity with the sense of isolation, the outlaw consciousness, the imminent danger of destruction and the desperate determination which they discovered in the revolutionary movement.

Finally, one should mention the fact that the proletarian writers, like their *bundan* counterparts, did not succeed in avoiding in their professional life the trap set for them by commercial journalism. In the Japanese literary world, where great importance is placed on the writer's private life, there is a danger, says Itō Sei, that even the desperate actions of revolutionary writers are subconsciously aimed at evoking a response from newspapers and magazines. A revolutionary act is the sort of performance which journalism likes to use and pays for handsomely. Meiji revolutionaries boasted about the number of times they had been jailed, and socialists in the Taishō period kept a watchful eye on the newspapers to see whether their actions were being reported. Furthermore, journalism has always tried to make these acts appear as violent as possible and thereby to increase their commercial value. And as far as literary men were concerned, there were a few examples at the beginning of the Shōwa period of writers throwing themselves into the ideological movement because they realised its high commercial value on the journalistic market. In this way the revolutionary movement could become a kind of performance. But although they were 'fighting theatrically', all the same they were persecuted and put into prison.[18]

In his essay 'Soshiki to ningen' (Organisation and Man) Itō Sei concludes that a Communist writer selling his writings was in the same position as the *bundan* writer. He fell prey to the monster of capitalistic journalism, which grew into a powerful organisation and the larger it grew the more restricting its demands on the writer's freedom became. In their rebellion against society and their search for freedom writers turned to journalism and this eventually resulted in a loss of freedom, as their criticism of society and their tendency to fight it created a commercial value in its sensationalism. For the Communist writer the loss of freedom was doubled by the fact that as Party members they were forced to support the Party line. Thus self-assertion again led towards a loss of self.

To sum up Itō Sei's view of the proletarian literary movement, it is his opinion that the way of thinking in Japanese literature did not change radically under the Marxist guise. The style and the emotional appeal of the revolutionary I-novel remained basically the same as that of the *bundan* I-novel. And it was just as difficult to understand to those who did not know anything about the author's way of life. Further, literary and artistic factors were usually ignored in favour of the moral problem of whether one's attitude within the movement was correct. As in the *bundan*, the works of proletarian literature were appraised by the other members of the movement according to the righteousness of the ideas and actions of the author, which remained largely incomprehensible to the general public.

The Marxist writer's postion *vis-à-vis* society was even weaker than that of the *bundan* writer. His isolation was deeper precisely because of his political convictions, and his view of society more limited. In a sense, he is an extreme counterpart of the *bundan* writer in his attitude towards life and literature. In his search for truth and purity in life, he was, as in the case of the *bundan* writer, alienated from his environment, and he adopted a literary method which enabled him to convey the pure quality of his life. The two fought each other as enemies, but their will to practise pure lives was the same. They were like 'two companions, closed from the world and competing with each other in the purer and higher form of life'.[19] They were both subject to the extreme pressures exerted on them by the reality of the social system: the I-novelist had to fight the anxieties, misery and emotions caused by his abandonment of society; the Marxist had to fight with the difficulties which his attitude of being an uncompromising revolutionary unavoidably invited – arrest, torture, treason and conversion. Both were exploited by journalism which threatened to transform their sincerely conceived ideals into a profitable enterprise.

CONCLUSION

When one thinks about the undoubted achievements of Japanese proletarian literature, Itō Sei's view seems to be partly biased, representing basically the *bundan* point of view. When it was formed in the Taishō period, the proletarian literary movement gathered under its banner all the anti-authoritarian, radical and progressive ideas of its time, and it grew as a revolutionary movement based on the idea of class struggle and social justice. It produced literary works through which, for the first time, modern Japanese literature reached a level of parity with some twentieth-century European literature. Works like Kobayashi Takiji's *Kani kōsen* or Nakano Shigeharu's *Harusaki no kaze* were translated into many languages and held up as paragons of revolutionary literature in many countries.

Naturally the movement had its weaknesses. Throughout its life it struggled with the theoretical difficulties of introducing Soviet artistic directives into Japan, where the literary traditions were very different. It also tended to view human misery as due solely to the injustice of the social and economic systems.

Its impact on Japanese literary life, however, cannot be over-emphasised. Its appearance is often seen as being of a magnitude comparable only to the rise of naturalism.

Proletarian literature opened new vistas for the *bundan* writers, who had exhausted the possibilities of individualism in the I-novel and *shinkyō shōsetsu*. It burst open the narrow subjective frame of the I-novel and showed the individual as a member of a social group or social class. It produced tragic figures like Arishima and Akutagawa who, unable to abandon their artistic ideas in favour of the new proletarian literature, were drawn towards its ideology by a force that they could only resist by death, but it also acquired many genuine sympathisers among socially-conscious writers.

Nevertheless, and here Itō Sei's argument strikes into the heart of the problem, because of their social isolation and high idealism, the proletarian writers were unable to produce literature which would reflect the reality of Japanese society. This was the paradox of their situation, that in spite of their aim of a broadly-based and socially-engaged literature, their art remained within the sphere of personal experience and practice, a tendency inherited from the I-novel.

In the light of the above remarks, it should not be surprising that, reflecting on the nature of modern Japanese literature, Itō Sei writes:

> In this way the main stream of modern Japanese literature becomes tied up with the personal experience of the writer. And I think that it is *this* aspect of the Japanese novel which must be appreciated if one is to grasp the special nature of Japanese prose-writing.[20]

It should also not be surprising that the reader who wants to learn through literature about the social problems and customs of the Japanese has to turn to *taishū bungaku* or popular mass literature. Popular literature developed in the Taishō period in opposition to the high-brow, personal *bundan* narrative, and was equally despised by both *bundan* and Marxist writers. Writers of popular literature by virtue of living inside the society created a popular fiction in which they succeeded in presenting the problems of common people. But they were no idealists; they were not concerned with changing society or fighting it. From the *bundan* point of view, their attitude was one of submission and compromise. They described the social reality in their works with the sole purpose of creating an entertaining literature. Not concerned with the purity of artistic standards they treated literature as a means of earning their livelihood – an attitude unacceptable to the *bundan*.

As will be seen in the following chapter, it was not proletarian literature but popular literature, which, supported by the growth of a mass society and a flourishing publishing industry, posed the greatest threat to the existence of the *bundan* in the Shōwa period.

7 Decline

The major developments in the history of the *bundan* took place in two great transitional periods in the history of modern Japan. The first, its beginning and end marked by the Sino-Japanese and Russo-Japanese wars, was the period of change between Meiji and Imperial Japan to which the origin of the *bundan* has been ascribed. The second, its beginning marked by the great Tokyo earthquake in 1923, opened the way to social and political changes which transformed Japan into a modern totalitarian State ready to take her part in the arena of international affairs. It is to this second period that the decline of the *bundan* may be ascribed. The late Taishō period and the early Shōwa period marked the beginning of the end of the *bundan* as a closed, sectarian society. This does not preclude the fact that literary critics, writers and publishers talk about the *bundan* even today: expressions such as the '*bundan* spirit' or a '*bundan* novel' or the '*bundan* hierarchy' still appear in literary jargon. But what they refer to are the qualities which constituted the essence of the pre-war *bundan* – an exclusive society devoted to the theory and practice of the pure novel.

This book has concentrated on an admittedly schematic presentation of the modes of thought and behaviour within the *bundan* from its beginnings in the Meiji era through the period of its full development in the Taishō era. By way of conclusion some factors which caused its decline in the Shōwa era will be mentioned, and this will be followed by an attempt at a general evaluation of the phenomenon of the *bundan* within modern Japanese literature.

The 'pure' way of life and the ideal of 'pure literature' exemplified by the *bundan* have gradually proved untenable against the pressures exerted by the fast developing reality of the modern Japanese State. As has been mentioned above, the epoch-making event in this period was the great Kantō earthquake of 1923, which destroyed down-town Tokyo. In Maruyama Masao's words: 'One cannot stress too strongly the social significance of the changes which occurred in all aspects of life after the earthquake in Tokyo, the capital representing, in a compressed fashion, the modernisation of Japan as a whole.'[1] Professor Maruyama quotes Yokomitsu Riichi who, after the earthquake, became the champion of a new literary movement called Shinkankakuha, describing the scene:

> To an unbelievable extent the great city was reduced to burnt ruins that stretched as far as one could see. In this burnt-out field the incarnation of speed, i.e. automobiles, appeared to wander about the streets, soon followed by the monster of sound called radio; then the model of birds, the airplane, began to fly in the sky for practical use. All of these are embodiments of modern science, coming forth in Japan one by one immediately after the earthquake disaster. . . .[2]

Thus the first result of the transformations which took place after the earthquake was radical progress in mechanisation and this changed the physical environment, in which the writers lived, in a concrete, tangible way. The beginning of radio broadcasting (1925), the proliferation of bars, cafés, the rapid development of tramway and suburban railway systems, the beginning of the subway system (1927), the growth of department stores and modern business offices – all these were *après-la-sismique* phenomena.[3] At about this time a new term *taishū bungei*, mass literature, was coined, giving expression to the changes which had occurred in the literary market. Popular monthly magazines were beginning to be sold in hundreds of thousands of copies, and also the *yenbon* (collections of famous novels, stories or poems priced at one yen each volume) which came into vogue after 1926, told dramatically of the great success of mass advertising. 'All events seemed to point to the full-fledged growth of "mass society" in a tiny, though central, part of the country.'[4]

The development of mass society and the hitherto unprecedented growth of journalism exerted a combined pressure on the *bundan* to give a social and popular dimension to the content of its literature, and as a final result destroyed effectively the structure of the *bundan* itself.

Nakamura Mitsuo has described the conditions which marked the beginning of the Shōwa literature as follows:

> What made Shōwa literature so different from its Taishō predecessor was the realisation on the writer's part that the times

when he could view his own individuality as absolute were gone, and that his mode of expression had to take others into account. These 'others' appeared to him in two forms. One was the mass of readers, different from those who read the *bundan* I-novel, who emerged as a result of the sudden appearance of popular literature and the general trend among writers to write newspaper novels. The other was 'society' in the sense that evolved during the development of proletarian literature. These two phenomena may seen at a first glance completely unrelated, but in fact they represented two aspects of the larger phenomenon of the socialisation of literature. And the problem of how writers were going to cope with this strong demand for both reality and ideals, which issued from the non-literary background, became the central spiritual dilemma of Shōwa literature, to which a solution has not yet been found even today.[5]

The *bundan* literature of the Meiji and Taishō periods, endlessly preoccupied with the 'self', 'individual' and 'human fate', was thrown into confusion by this confrontation with a completely alien concept of 'society', and this marked the beginnings of Shōwa literature. When writers turned their attention to the problem of the 'socialisation of literature' they had available to them the two models of *taishū bungaku* or popular mass literature and proletarian literature.

The proletarian postulate for the socialisation of literature remained largely a theoretical consideration. Although Kobayashi Takiji dreamed of an equal popularity for his works as that enjoyed by *taishū bungaku*, his hopes, for reasons which should be evident from the earlier discussion of the proletarian movement, remained largely unfulfilled.

TAISHŪ BUNGAKU

It was *taishū bungaku* whose powerful presence from the end of the Taishō period formed the literary backbone of the new mass society. *Taishū bungaku* developed in response to the ideas of Taishō democracy and proclaimed 'art for the people' as its platform. Its aim was to become a genuine 'national' literature that would express the sentiments of Japanese people from various walks of life. When it began, it was as opposed to the cheap modern fiction sponsored by the mass media, the so-called *tsūzoku shōsetsu* (popular novel), as to the *bundan* literature. That it responded to a real spiritual need of the people was proved by its explosive popularity. The following contrasting statistics illustrate the comparative success of *taishū bungaku* in its early days: *yenbon* booklets were regularly published in runs of more than 400,000 copies, while the proletarian magazine *Senki* reached at the time of its greatest popularity 30,000 copies and the pure literature magazine *Shinchō* rarely exceeded 5,000 copies.[6]

The early socialist Nakazato Kaizan (1885–1944) is usually considered a precursor of *taishū bungaku* as his work, the historical romance *Daibosatu Toge* (Daibosatsu Pass, 1918–1941), was a best seller. Nakazato himself stood aloof from the *bundan* and from the mass media, leading a lonely life devoted to popular education. The fact that his works were read and liked by the mass of the people was incompatible with the dignity of the *bundan* writer, and he was firmly designated as a writer of the popular camp.

Shirai Kyōji (1889–) who in 1925 founded a coterie magazine entitled *Taishū bungei*, became the leader of the *taishū bungaku* movement. Around him gathered writers like Naoki Sanjūgo, Edogawa Ranpō (the name is a corruption of Edgar Allan Poe), Yoshikawa Eiji and Osaragi Jirō, who produced literature rich in imagination and full of interest for the readers: historical romances, stories for the young, humorous novels and works of fiction on political subjects. In 1927 the first collected works of the *taishū bungaku* writers were published. The series was entitled *Gendai taishū bungaku zenshū*, and from this time the term '*taishū bungaku*' entered common use.

For a few years *taishū bungaku* preserved its distinction from the popular *tsūzoku shōsetsu*, but from about 1930 the movement was gradually taken over by the mass media and the difference became blurred. The *taishū* writers began writing novels on modern domestic themes, love stories and detective stories, which up till then had been the domain of *tsūzoku shōsetsu*. The serious and genuine efforts of the *taishū* writers to create a national literature were stifled by the power of commercial journalism, and the term '*taishū bungaku*' became a symbol of popular literature written for entertainment of the masses. *Taishū bungaku* was now a commercial product meant for mass production and mass consumption.

In response to the demands of journalism for material that would appeal to a wider circle of readers, there appeared inside the *bundan* itself a large number of writers who transferred their allegiance from pure to popular literature. The most famous figure among them was Kikuchi Kan (1888–1948). Aware of the reality of mass society and the power of commercial journalism, Kikuchi Kan and the group of writers who gathered round him, concentrated their efforts on raising the standards of popular literature. By preserving the professional standards and at the same time socialising the content of the novel, Kikuchi planned to create a literature of general interest and thus use the phenomenon of the commercialisation of literature as a means to establish some relative independence for the *bundan* . He spared no effort to protect the writers' interests and their professional incomes, and to raise their living standards. He initiated several organisations concerned with writers' welfare and instituted a system of literary prizes – the Naoki Prize, Kikuchi Kan Prize, Akutagawa Prize – to help young writers. He became the 'grand old man' of the pre-war *bundan* (*bundan no ōgosho*). His activity was directed towards leading the *bundan* away from its élitist position towards the integration of writers as a professional group into the reality of modern life.

BUNDAN AND JOURNALISM

The factor that more than anything else conspired against the isolationism of the *bundan* and the idealistic attitudes of the *bundan* writers was the growth of journalism into a large and powerful institution. Itō Sei writes that journalism at the beginning of the Shōwa period became so highly organised and powerful that the freedom it once offered to writers became transformed into constraint, while writers who formerly wrote for pennies began to receive disproportionately high sums. This situation, which persists to this day, resulted in a loss of freedom and created an anxiety about the future of pure literature. Writers were no longer fugitive slaves or outcasts, but they were now at the mercy of a complex publishing machine. They could not survive professionally outside this organisation and the result was that instead of creating works in accordance with their consciences, they were only allowed to create products which suited mass taste, by which they were ruled.[7]

In *Kappa* Akutagawa Ryūnosuke describes a publishing house where brain pulp goes into the machines at one end and the ready made works appear at the other. Journalism posed the threat that *bundan* efforts towards socialisation of the novel would achieve nothing but a cheap popularisation, which would amount to a betrayal of freedom.

In historical terms, journalism had given modern Japanese writers an opportunity to advance in the world (*risshin shusse*). But in the Meiji and Taishō periods, when journalism was still relatively small in scale, writers had been living outside the bureaucratic structure of society in abandonment and misery. In the Shōwa period, although they have still preserved their consciousness of being outlaws, they have in fact become a part of the journalistic and publishing industries. Living their lives within the powerful structure of those organisations, they have gradually become fully-fledged members of society, sensible citizens who take care of their families and send their children to the universities. But their freedom of speech and action has become severely limited.[8]

The *bundan* guild which emerged at the end of the Meiji period to protect the professional standards of literature and the living standards of the writers lost its *raison d'être* as journalism usurped its functions. The close and tangible human relations inside the *bundan* broke down, and at the same time its spiritual unity was destroyed. Writers could no longer spend their lives completely within the *bundan*, ruled by the *bundan* ethics, ignoring society; the number of *bundan*-oriented lives declined sharply.

Ōya Sōichi, a left-wing critic, first indicated the demise of the *bundan* in an article written at the very end of the Taishō period entitled 'Bundan girudo no kaitaiki' (The Time of the Disintegration of the *Bundan* Guild, 1926). This article formulates a theory of the *bundan* as a guild organisation and analyses the destructive influence that the growth of journalism had on it.

In Ōya's view, the social structure of the *bundan* resembled closely the medieval craft guilds. It was built on the existence of the master (the *bundan oyagata*) and his disciples who were the apprentices in the craft. It was based on the apprenticeship system and, like the medieval guilds, it observed strictly the distinction between the professionals and the amateurs. If one did not spend years in apprenticeship learning the discipline, one remained, in the eyes of the *bundan*, an amateur.

The *shuppan kinenkai* party[9] was the modern equivalent of the graduation ceremony in the old guilds, at which the new member produced the masterpiece that he hoped would ensure his success. It celebrated the entrance of a new member into the *bundan*. His graduation product did not have to be a real masterpiece; it only indicated the fact that he had a master who guaranteed his craftsmanship and who was giving the party for him. From that moment the young member's aim was to become famous, which in the *bundan* terminology meant to become a 'master'. Thus, before one could write a praiseworthy work one had to have a master and friends who would confer that praise. The *bundan* was a gathering of friends who supported and praised each other. The platitudes of the literary critics, who 'praise the master', 'praise the pupil' and 'praise his fellow writers', spoke eloquently about the nature of *bundan* relationships. The *bundan* that had existed up to this point had been formed from a conglomeration of guilds: the 'I-novel guild', the 'drama guild', '*tsūzoku* guild', '*taishū* guild', etc.

Secondly, as was the case with the medieval guild, the *bundan* had the power to monopolise the market, thus hindering free market competition. It protected its product and was a social organisation, which once joined, offered lifelong protection and security to its members.

In the second part of the article Ōya describes the effects of journalism on the guild's life. Journalism created a wide circle of readers and literary 'fans' (in the same way as there were sports fans), who could transform even the most worthless literary work into a highly-priced commodity. As a result the social position of writers rose abruptly, and literary aspirants now started appearing even from the bureaucracy. Writers who had been until recently very poorly paid, now went by taxi to geisha parties. But the literature that resulted from the lives led by these writers (which consisted mainly of love affairs, liaisons with geisha and bar waitresses, games of cards, *mah-jong* and *shōgi*) was a literature of dissipation. As the *bundan* struggled to preserve its control over the market by supporting such works, it introduced into itself an element of its own destruction.

Ōya points out the inevitable drop in the quality of literary works associated with the growth of journalism: works of literature no longer carried the ethical message which they had in the past, and while the guild had cared about the quality of its product, journalism did not. The distinction between the professional and the amateur disappeared, as any work of interest to the reader could sell well on the market. Ōya finds the *bundan* in a state of confusion: the pure literature magazines had to popularise themselves to survive financially, and the idea of pure literature was being challenged by new ways of social thinking and by new literary fashions copied from abroad. The *bundan* writers were responding either by joining the commercial world or by withdrawal from reality deep into the *bundan*, but their fate would be the same as that of the *samurai* class after the Meiji Restoration – disintegration. It is indeed surprising, Ōya concludes, that the guild has survived so far under the conditions of a capitalist economy.[10]

One can only admire Ōya Sōichi's insight into events whose meaning only became clear twenty or thirty years later. At a very early stage he perceived the elements of the new situation which caused the eventual decline of the *bundan*. Later writers and critics with all the experience of hindsight could only develop and confirm his ideas.

THE PRE-WAR AND WAR-TIME *BUNDAN*

The new young generation of *bundan* writers that grew up amidst the social turmoil of the late Taishō and early Shōwa years could no longer accept the I-novel as the ideal of modern fiction. With the gradual disintegration of the *bundan* and the socialisation of the writers' lives, the I-novel, whose topic was the *bundan* way of life, lost its meaning. The confession of the I-novelist lost the ethical value it derived from the writer exposing his very existence to danger and developing his art through years of hardship. Deprived of its positive rebellious character, the I-novel lost its original function and became merely a technique, a symbol of opportunism rather than opposition, resembling popular literature in spirit.

The I-novels, which continued to appear well into the post-war period, showed a shift from nihilistic resignation into an easy-going affirmation of reality. They were written by writers who took care of their families and were responsible members of society. The I-novelist Kawasaki Chotarō is a case in point. His works achieved great journalistic popularity after the war, but the degree of truth of his confessions was clearly circumscribed by the author's anxiety about preserving the stability of his family life. Written in such a frame of mind, the I-novel, completely deprived of its protest value, lost its emotional appeal and was pushed aside into a corner of the literary world. The disintegration of the *bundan* and the weakness of the I-novel are related phenomena. Writers whose lives were no longer limited to the *bundan* and ruled by the *bundan* ethics lost interest in the narrow confessional I-novel and sought new literary methods which would reflect the new reality of their lives. In the early Shōwa period they looked for models in the European and American post-First World War literature.

In Itō Sei's view the search for a new style was the natural reaction of the *bundan* to the changed situation in Japan:

It is normal for a sudden change to occur in literary style at a time when the social order is shaken and revolutionary ideas appear. Literary style became colloquial and realistic in time with the modernisation of ideas in the 1880s and at the end of the Meiji period. At the end of the Taishō and the beginning of the Shōwa period, when Marxism was in vogue, the hitherto calm colloquial style was destroyed by a group of writers not uninfluenced by the First World War in Europe, of whom the principal figure was Yokomitsu Riichi. A new style was born which depended on the concentration of vibrant impressions and this was described by the term 'new impressionism'. This was in opposition to the logic of the colloquial style up to that time. In terms of the *bundan* consciousness the literary style of this period is explained as a confrontation between Marxist literature with its political thought and New Impressionist [Shinkankakuha] literature with its emphasis on the primacy of art. It is true that Marxist ways of thinking also penetrated the New Impressionist School, and that New Impressionist technique was also taken up by the Marxists, but in the end there was a clear confrontation between them.

It seems correct to say that these two manifestations were simply a reflection of the single phenomenon of the disturbance in the social order. At the time when the normal logic of Japanese society, as expressed in its colloquial literary style, was being disturbed, writers who had an interest in literary style sought for one which . . . was consistent with the new modes of thought.[11]

At about the same time Kobayashi Hideo wrote *Shishōsetsu ron* (On the I-novel, 1935) and suggested a new way of individualism in the form of a 'socialised self' (*shakaika shita watakushi*). This was an attempt to find a solution to the dilemma of the 'artistic school' represented by the I-novel and the new modernistic movements by taking into account the ideas coming from the 'social school' represented by the proletarian and popular mass literary movements. Itō Sei himself followed Kobayashi's precepts in the novels which he wrote during the war and in the post-war period.[12]

Unfortunately, a new realism did not have much chance of survival in the Japan of the 1930s because of the severe suppression of the whole intellectual movement at the time. Again the career of Yokomitsu Riichi may serve as an illustration:

> Yokomitsu Riichi was the writer who created the style of Shinkankakuha. His work *Kikai* (Machine, 1930) represents a consolidation of that style and led in the logical direction of the novel of psychological analysis. This was a correct direction to take. But he gave it up half way and diverted the logic of this style into a mode of thought which seemed to give approval to the feudal morality of Japanese society. This was in a time of war and it was an inevitable step for him to take as he was a representative writer who would be watched. . . . To approve of the reality of Japan in the war he had to adopt this mode of thought which forced upon him a dogmatic, illogical and painful spiritual life and made his life-consciousness shrink. He lived like a fasting man who would not recognise modern medical care. The case of Yokomitsu Riichi reflects Japanese ethical and religious modes of thought which assume that through self-abandonment and self-sacrifice justice will be accomplished.[13]

The element of self-denial and withdrawal noted by Itō Sei in the attitude of Yokomitsu Riichi during the later part of his life became, with the approach of the war, an undercurrent of Shōwa literature, both that proclaiming the primacy of art as well as that of Marxist orientation.

In this case also the great earthquake marked the turning point. With it came the end of Taishō liberalism, which had been beneficial to the independence of the *bundan*. Maruyama Masao mentions the brutal slaughter of Osugi Sakae and prominent trade union activists in the turmoil of the earthquake disaster, the simultaneous enactment of the Universal Manhood Suffrage Act and of the Peace Preservation Act (1925), the prohibition of 'social study groups' in many universities and colleges, and the mass arrest of communists and left-wing sympathisers, called the March Fifteen Incident (1928), as epoch-making events following the great earthquake one after another.[14]

According to Maruyama the changes in the social and political situation in the period following the great earthquake gave rise to a type of 'atomised individual' (as opposed to the 'privatised' individual behaviour that brought to life the I-novel):

He is a person who suffers bitterly from the actual or imagined state of uprootedness and the loss of norms of conduct (anomie). The feeling of loneliness, anxiety, fear, and frustration brought about by the precipitous change of his environment characterises his psychology. The atomised individual is usually apathetic to public affairs, but sometimes this very apathy will turn abruptly into fanatic participation in politics. Just because he is concerned with escaping from loneliness and insecurity, he is inclined to identify himself totally with authoritarian leadership or to submerge himself into the mystical 'whole' expressed in such ideas as national community, eternal racial culture, etc.

The atomised attitude differs greatly from privatisation, which was characteristic of the previous period of modernisation in Japan. In the case of privatisation, the scope of interest is rather confined to one's 'private' affairs and is not as floating as that of atomisation. Psychologically, the apathetic attitude of the privatised individual is more stable than that of the atomised individual, who is oscillating between over-politicisation and utter apathy. In Maruyama's view, in the period after the great earthquake, a shift from privatisation to atomisation of attitudes took place on a grand scale, particularly after the onset of the Great Depression in 1929, which produced a huge number of unemployed labourers, intellectuals and white-collar workers. Considering the political situation in Japan at the time, it is not surprising that the increase in atomisation not so much favoured the leftist movement as paved the way for ultra-nationalist tendencies.[15]

When one looks at the literary scene from the perspective of Professor Maruyama's definition, it seems to present a picture which confirms his theory.

The proletarian literary movement was brutally suppressed and the proletarian writers were forced into conversion (*tenkō*). With few exceptions the converts either sank into nihilistic despair and apathy or transferred their allegiance to the current imperialistic political ideology. In the former case popular fiction on modern urban manners or I-novels reflecting the atmosphere of decadence and degeneration, full of self-scorn, like Takami Jun's *Kokyū wasureubeki* (Must One Forget the Old Friends, 1936), appeared. In a broad sense even Dazai Osamu's *Dōke no hana* (Flowers of the Clown, 1935), although a typical example of the self-destructive histrionic nature of his literature, is nevertheless a product of the failure of the proletarian movement.[16] In the latter, romantic novels turning to Japan's past and glorifying the imperial tradition were produced.

No longer did the increasingly powerful totalitarian regime treat the *bundan* writers with indifference. It was inconceivable to leave uncontrolled such a dangerous lacuna of liberty as was represented by the *bundan*, which offered writers a place of escape from the requirement of complete dedication to the State demanded by the prevailing ultra-nationalist ideology.

The authorities classed the passive attitude of the *bundan* writers in the same category as the active resistance of the socialists. It was significant that in the Imperial Rescript for the Promotion of the National Spirit (1924) 'frivolous radical tendencies' and the 'habit of luxurious indulgence' were linked together as the two prevalent patterns of subversive life-style. As Bernard Crick has shown, to the totalitarian regime not merely the machinery of the government and the economic institutions of society, but also education, art, even domesticity and private affection, all these, both in work and leisure, are part of a completely interrelated social system; all are forces which must be accountable to the ideology.[17]

The Japanese literary intelligentsia was facing the darkest period of its history. Having witnessed the suppression of radical thought they were overwhelmed with a feeling of powerlessness and hate towards the mechanism of society. They lost the ethical base on which their art and lives were founded; they lost their belief in the reality of literature; they suffered from a loss of self-confidence and a sense of uprootedness and found themselves in a spiritual vacuum, experiencing only frustration, anxiety and crisis. The tragic fate of Yokomitsu Riichi was a symbol of this age. The literature of self-denial and the literature of guilty conscience became the literature of the day.

The writers who were determined to defend the high standards of pure literature could only follow the old route of withdrawal from reality into the world of aestheticism, and many accepted this route as the only way in which they could manifest their protest against the attack on the freedom of literature. On the other hand the effort to socialise the novel was accompanied by a feeling of guilty conscience on the part of the writers because it could not be distinguished from popularisation. Since it was impossible to publish anything which would convey an unveiled criticism of the real situation, only innocent novels of social manners and customs could develop. However skilfully writers began to use materials which had a definite connection with real society, their novels tended all the more towards popular literature.

As the war began (1937), the spiritual isolation of the writers increased as evidence of the power of the State to interfere directly in literature mounted. Many writers were mobilised into the so-called '*pen butai*' or pen brigade, which was divided into two units, one accompanying the army and the other the navy. In the occupied territories such writers were forced to co-operate with the army's occupation policies.

The writers at home not only had to suffer material hardships – column space in the newspapers and magazines was limited, and the quantity of paper allotted to literary works decreased – but they also had to endure a systematic suppression of their freedom. With the establishment of the Board of Information (1940) control over thought and subject matter reached its climax. Some writers were prohibited from writing, others like Nagai Kafū declined the opportunity to appear in print. Nothing which could 'corrupt good manners, or described any immoral conduct' could be published. Even the works of such literary elders as Tanizaki Jun'ichirō or Tokudo Shūsei, not to mention many others, were banned from newspapers and magazines. The publishing organisation Nihon Shuppan Bunka Kyōkai was responsible to the Board of Information and pre-censorship of all published material was established. The pressure exerted by the authorities which aimed at centralising and controlling the activities of the *bundan*, culminated in the formation of the Nihon Bungaku Hōkokukai (Patriotic Association of Japanese Literature, 1942), which was directly supervised by the Board of Information. The independence of the literary world ceased at this point. Writers withdrew into their private lives where in isolated self-confinement they awaited the end of the war.

CONCLUSION

To sum up the character of the changes which occurred in the Japanese literary world in the Shōwa period: it seems that there were four important factors which influenced the *bundan* and caused its decline:

1. The radicalisation of social movements after the First World War, and the development of Marxism and Marxist-oriented 'proletarian literature'.
2. The growth of a mass society and the emergence of popular mass literature (*taishū bungaku*).
3. The rapid development of journalism and the publishing industry, which accompanied the rise of mass society and which was beginning to use the techniques of mass production in response to its demands.
4. The over-sensitive response of the increasingly totalitarian government to every show of marked individualism and the enforcement of preventive measures against 'subversive tendencies'.

The combined effects of those four factors influenced the *bundan* way of life and thought in two basic ways:

(1) The *bundan* experienced a sense of crisis, confusion and anxiety over the future of literature. The view of the I-novel as an ideal form of literature disappeared, and the distinction between pure and popular literature became blurred as the writers searched for material in their surroundings in their effort to socialise the novel. The subjects of politics, society, customs and ideology entered modern Japanese literature for the first time in the Shōwa period giving at a character quite distinct when compared with previous periods. Great literary disputes on the social role and artistic importance of literature swept the *bundan* and after the interruption of the war continued into the post-war period.

(2) The social position of the writers changed and the *bundan* lost its character as a community of escaping slaves. If anything, it became a miniature of the real world. With the changes that took place in the composition and character of the reading public, with the relative decline of imaginative written literature in favour either of other forms of expression or other media, and with the fading of a clearly defined and selective notion of 'high' or 'pure' literature – with all these trends, the social conditions that made literary élitism an effective possibility disappeared and the situation of the writers changed. Shōwa writers lost the missionary ideal, directed against the utilitarian reality, of a unity of life and art – an ideal for which

the *bundan* writers in the Taishō period had sacrificed the comfort of their lives. They accepted society and conceived their role from within it. What the writers had to consider from then onwards, and what re-emerged strongly in the post-war discussion on literature, was the destiny of the writer in a mass society.

The disintegration of the *bundan* was welcomed by its critics who saw in it a feudal type of organisation incompatible with the modern way of life. Such was the message of the article by Oya Sōichi mentioned earlier and such was the essence of the well-known criticism of the *bundan* published after the war by the social scientist Hidaka Rokuro. Hidaka talked about the narrow *bundan* guild, the *oyabun–kobun* relationships, about the *bundan* as a gathering of outlaws, about the special *bundan* morality and special relationships with publishers.[18] But as was pointed out to him by *bundan* men like Ara Masahito and Togaeri Hajime, he was in fact criticising the *bundan* of the past. When he wrote his article, the *bundan* that he was describing, no longer existed.

The literary critic Togaeri Hajime expressed his views in his famous ' "Bundan" hokai ron' (Treatise on the Destruction of the '*Bundan*', 1956):

Today we use the term *bundan* out of convenience, although it no longer indicates the real *bundan*. What is expressed by the use of the word *bundan* today is no more than a literary aspect of journalism. In other words it is the journalism and not the *bundan* that has become the reality of our lives.[19]

The submergence of the *bundan* into journalism, writes Togaeri, brought the writers freedom from the guild rules. To publish or to write today it is no longer necessary to knock at the master's gate or to receive his blessing. If the work is considered interesing on account of its topic, even though it is not of a high artistic value, the literary magazines immediately ask the writer for a manuscript. Such writers are received by journalism as 'novelists' and begin to inhabit the same social sphere as the professionals, the *bundan* writers.

The *bundan* as a training ground for young writers has disappeared. Until recently, young writers, before they became known in society, had to spend years of their life in obscurity, learning from their elders and friends and absorbing the *bundan* ethics, which differed from the general moral standards of society.

The phrase '*kusetsu jūnen*' ('ten years of unswerving loyalty') described this type of training which emphasised the experience of poverty, illness and suffering caused by a woman as necessary elements of the discipline of the first-rate writer. Today, however, writers have to face the reality that the literary concepts which they learnt from their elders are of no use to them as writers. Today many works are published by young authors who do not know such hardship and even despise it. Their works have a high commercial value and are welcomed by the reader. A record of ten or twenty years of hardship learning to write novels has no meaning when faced with such a phenomenon. The *bundan* ethic has been completely defeated. These young writers do not learn from hardship, or from their elders. They learn from the reality of their lives, which is the normal way of life of Japanese youth today. The 'literary masters' do not exist in their lives; they are not '*bungaku seinen*' (literary youths, literary aspirants) in the old sense. For them the *bundan* does not exist.

Their existence is due to journalism which forms an integral part of their lives. Their literature is a product of this life, and this suggests an inevitable change in the character of literary art today. Writers have to write with large audiences in mind, particularly so since radio, television and film have become the means through which writers can express their ideas. They can no longer write things understandable only to themselves, as they no longer spend their lives within the enclosure of the *bundan*.[20]

The *bundan* literary critics, although on the whole welcoming the dissolution of the restrictive guild, nevertheless instinctively deplored the *bundan*'s loss of identity *vis-à-vis* journalism, which they feared would bring down literary standards and establish the commercial value of a literary work as the ultimate criterion.

The case that clearly illustrated to them the powerless position of the *bundan* was that of Ishihara Shintarō, a young novelist of the new generation whose work *Taiyō no kisetsu* (Sunny Season, 1955) in spite of protests from the *bundan*, received the Akutagawa literary prize. Completely ignoring the opinion expressed by the *bundan*, journalism transformed Ishihara into a commercial star. If one compares that event with the situation of some thirty years earlier, when Akutagawa Ryūnosuke publicly warned the *Chūō kōron* magazine against publishing his work in the same issue as the work of the *taishū* writer Muramatsu Shōfu, the dramatic change that took place in the relationship between the *bundan* and journalism becomes evident. The *bundan* always relied on journalism for its life support, but while in the Taishō period it stood in a position of some authority against journalism over literary policies, in the Shōwa period it has lost that authority to the detriment of the literature itself.

This society of love and trust for literature, which could not be readily understood by outsiders, as Nakajima Kenzō once defined the *bundan*, has gone and there is a danger that if the God of commercialism prevails literary standards will decline and true literature will face annihilation. Such were the fears of the post-war *bundan*.

Itō Sei took up another aspect of contemporary literature, no longer protected by the existence of the *bundan*. He deplored the loss of the freedom of the individual in a modern society, which he saw both as a general social development and as something which affected the arts in particular. Modern man has lost the privilege, he argued, of possessing his own views; he belongs to a large organisation and is obliged to represent its view rather than his own. Itō Sei questioned the possibility of freedom in literature and freedom for the writer within the context of an organisation as big and powerful as journalism had become:

I learned from my own bitter experience, living in that organisation, that within the journalistic world, which should be most conscientious and most free of all, nothing which might be called freedom exists. The time when art flourishes and the artist is rich is the time when he is the least free. In the Meiji and Taishō periods, our predecessors escaped from the old inhuman institutions of society and State. They created the *bundan* which closed its eyes on society, and in which even the family institution hardly functioned, so small and poor the *bundan* was. In those days our predecessors were free, but their freedom was synonymous with rejection, suicide and misery. Today, one might say that many writers have a comfortable life, conducting successfully the business of selling their novels. But it relies mainly on supplying an entertaining kind of literature to the never satiated literary market. And there is always a danger that some political or business organisation will restrict or expel a writer or make use of him for its own purposes.[21]

There is a pessimistic tone to Itō Sei's observations. The development of modern literature clearly did not fulfil the hopes of the early founders of the *bundan*. On the contrary, the hopes for the self-establishment of a free and independent individual, on which modern Japanese literature was founded and for which the *bundan* writers paid with their lives, have been dashed by modern mass society. The destiny of a successful writer in a mass society, writes Itō Sei, is destruction of the self rather than its assertion. As soon as the writer achieves recognition, the commercial or political value of his work creates circumstances in which his integrity is threatened or destroyed. He becomes a cog in an organisation and has to follow its rules.[22]

Those who wish well to Japanese literature, and the great art of novel writing in general, cannot but applaud the spirit which underlies Itō Sei's criticism:

I wished to question the premise of the argument, widely believed today, that the writer or the artist is free. The very discovery of how much we lack freedom may itself bring us a little closer to real freedom.[23]

Notes

General remarks
The references to Japanese books will follow the Japanese practice of mentioning the author's surname before his given name. As almost all Japanese books are published in Tokyo, only the publisher's name will be given.

Notes to the Introduction

1. Milton C. Albrecht, 'Art as an Institution', in Milton C. Albrecht, James M. Barnett and Meson Griff (eds), *Sociology of Art and Literature: A Reader* (London: Gerald Duckworth, 1970).
2. R. Wellek and A. Warren, *Theory of Literature* (Harmondsworth: Penguin Books, 1978).
   See the chapter on 'Literature and Sociology', pp. 95–6.
3. G. A. Huaco, 'The Sociological Model', in Milton C. Albrecht *et al.* (eds), op. cit.
4. L. Goldmann, 'The Sociology of Literature', in Milton C. Albrecht *et al.* (eds), op. cit.
5. For further information on this subject see below, chapter 6.
6. For further information on this subject see below, chapters 2 and 3.
7. Kamei Hideo, *Itō Sei no sekai* (Kodansha, 1969).

Notes to Chapter One: The Meiji Literary World

1. The term 'Meiji Japan' is used here as defined by M. B. Jansen in M. B. Jansen (ed.), *Changing Japanese Attitudes toward Modernisation* (Princeton, N. J.: Princeton University Press, 1969) (referred to hereafter as *Changing Attitudes*) p. 77, to describe the period in Japanese history between the Restoration and 1900. It does not cover the whole of the actual Meiji period, which ended in 1912, but it was around 1900 that, according to Jansen, the distinctive character of Japan as a modern state became clearly recognisable. What emerged at this time established the nation's course during the next period of 'Imperial Japan' – a period that lasted until defeat at the end of the Second World War.
2. J. Hall, 'Changing Conceptions of the Modernization of Japan', in M. B. Jansen (ed.), *Changing Attitudes*, pp. 23–4.
3. M. Bradbury, *The Social Context of Modern English Literature* (Oxford: Basil Blackwell, 1971) pp. 9–11.

4. For a detailed description of the various types of popular literature in the Tokugawa period, see D. Keene, *World within Walls* (London: Secker & Warburg, 1976).
5. Ibid., p. 397.
6. According to Keene a change occurred in that system in the late Edo period: 'In the event the book was successful the publisher made additional payment to the author, thus anticipating the modern system of advance and royalties' (ibid., p. 410).
7. Calligraphy was one of the traditionally acknowledged skills and people who possessed this ability were often employed as professional letter writers.
8. Itō Sei, *Bungei tokuhon*, in *Itō Sei zenshū* (Collected Works of Itō Sei), vol. 17 (Shinchosha, 1973) pp. 145–50. As most quotations used here are taken from this edition of his collected works, the latter will be referred to hereafter simply as *Zenshū*.
9. Kosaka Masaaki, *Japanese Thought in the Meiji Era* (Pan–Pacific Press, 1958) p. 54.
10. M. Ryan, *Japan's First Modern Novel* (New York: Columbia University Press, 1967) p. 64.
11. Itō Sei, *Bungei tokuhon*, in *Zenshū*, vol. 17, pp. 147–53.
12. The term comes from Tokutomi Sohō's book *Shin Nihon no seinen* (New Japanese Youth) which was published in 1887 and aroused much interest among the young generation. The same year Tokutomi Sohō also founded a society, called the *Min'yūsha*, which started publishing a magazine *Kokumin no tomo* (Friend of the People) devoted to the propagation of the early Meiji ideals of democracy and individualism. With many intellectuals and young writers contributing to the magazine it became a focus of Meiji cultural life.
13. The novel has recently been translated into English by K. Strong under the title *Footprints in the Snow* (London: George Allen & Unwin, 1971).
14. K. Pyle, *The New Generation in Meiji Japan: Problems of Cultural Identity 1885–1895* (Stanford, Cal.: Stanford University Press, 1969) p. 78.
15. Maruyama Masao, 'Patterns of Individuation', in M. B. Jansen (ed.), *Changing Attitudes*, p. 510.
16. According to Chie Nakane, the relationship between two individuals of upper and lower status forms the basic structural principle of Japanese society and gives it its traditionally vertical character. The relationship between master and his disciple, or between the university professor, his assistants and his students, is constructed along a vertical line. 'The professor is closer to his assistant and to his students than he is to any of his fellow professors' – Chie Nakane, *Japanese Society* (London: Weidenfeld & Nicolson, 1970) p. 38.
17. Chie Nakane, ibid., p. 118.
18. Hirotsu Kazuo, whose father Hirotsu Ryūrō was a member of the Kōyō mon, mentions in his memoirs *Nengetsu no ashioto* (Kodansha, 1969) Izumi Kyōka, Oguri Fūyō, Yanagawa Shun'yō, Tayama Katai and Tokuda Shūsei as Kōyō's *shosei*. Hirotsu Ryūrō had his own *shosei* and students, one of whom, for a time, was Nagai Kafū.
19. Itō Sei, 'Rise of Naturalism', *Japan Quarterly*, vol. 2, no. 4 (1955) p. 510.
20. The incident is mentioned in Hirotsu Kazuo's memoirs, *Nengetsu no ashioto*, p. 41.
21. Chie Nakane, op. cit., p. 42.
22. Itō Sei, *Kyūdōsha to ninshikisha* (Shinchosha, 1962) p. 159.
23. The phenomenon of 'cliquishness' is also mentioned by Ivan Morris in his introduction to *Modern Japanese Stories*, ed. Ivan Morris (Tokyo: Charles E.

Tuttle, 1962) p. 17: 'The tendency of writers and others to band together in groups or societies derives directly from the pre-modern period, when the individual young artist had scant chance of recognition unless he could be identified with some established family or school that would give him its protection and encouragement. This relates to the feudal tradition of a close relationship between master and pupil, which even today plays an important part in literature and other fields.'

24. Maruyama Masao, *Nihon no shisō* (Iwanami Shinsho, 1961) p. 129.
25. K. Pyle, *The New Generation in Meiji Japan*, p. 15.
26. Itō Sei, *Shōsetsu no hōhō* (Kawade Shobo, 1956) p. 81:
27. Gaigo Gakkō – Tokyo School of Foreign Languages. The Russian department of the School had originated as a part of the Institute for the Training of Official Interpreters, founded during the Tokugawa regime. At the school some of the students were granted scholarships. In the Russian department most of the instructors were Russian, and the courses offered were almost the same as those taught in Russian secondary schools. All subjects were taught in Russian.
28. Nakamura Mitsuo, *Modern Japanese Fiction*, vol. 1 (Kokusai Bunka Shinkōkai, 1968) p. 42.
29. Quoted by Odagiri Hideo, *Bungakushi* (Tōkyō Keizai Shinpōsha, 1969) p. 150.
30. M. Ryan, *Japan's First Novel*, p. 147.
31. Itō Sei, *Shōsetsu no hōhō*, p. 81.
32. Uchida Roan, *Bungakusha to naru hō*, in *Gendai Nihon bungaku zenshū*, vol. 41 (Kaizōsha, 1930) pp. 376–436.
33. Itō Sei, *Shōsetsu no hōhō*, p. 81.
34. One of the famous maxims enunciated by General Araki Sadao, quoted by Maruyama Masao in *Thought and Behaviour in Modern Japanese Politics* (London: Oxford University Press, 1963) p. 8.
35. Fukutake Tadashi, *Man and Society in Japan* (The University of Tokyo Press, 1962) chapter 1, passim.
36. Itō Sei, *Shōsetsu no hōhō*, pp. 196–7.

Notes to Chapter Two: Naturalist 'Avant-garde' and the Formation of the Modern 'Bundan'

1. H. Passin, 'Modernisation and the Japanese Intellectual', in M. B. Jansen (ed.), *Changing Attitudes*, p. 480.
2. One can observe a similar changing social pattern in the literary communities. While the 1880s were still dominated by the writers of *samurai* origin (Tsubouchi Shōyō, Futabatei Shimei, Mori Ōgai, etc.), many of the *Bungakukai* writers in the 1890s either came from Tokyo *shitamachi* (downtown) merchant families, or lived in the Nihonbashi–Kyōbashi districts (the down-town shopping areas of Tokyo), such as Higuchi Ichiyō; the naturalist writers of the 1900s were mainly of country origin. Nagai Kafū in his polemical debates with the leading naturalist critic and writer Masamune Hakuchō in 1926 called him an 'unlettered rustic'.
3. H. Passin, 'Modernisation and the Japanese Intellectual', in M. B. Jansen (ed.), *Changing Attitudes*, p. 470.
4. Katō Shūichi, 'Japanese Writers and Modernisation', in M. B. Jansen (ed.), *Changing Attitudes*, p. 426.

5. Maruyama Masao, 'Patterns of Individuation', in M. B. Jansen (ed.), *Changing Attitudes*, p. 498.
6. Ibid., p. 508.
7. K. Pyle, *The New Generation in Meiji Japan*, pp. 183–99.
8. R. Williams, *The Long Revolution* (New York: Harper & Row, 1966) p. 109.
9. M. Bradbury, *The Social Context of Modern English Literature*, pp. 17–18.
10. Arima Tatsuo, *The Failure of Freedom: a Portrait of Modern Japanese Intellectuals* (Cambridge, Mass.: Harvard University Press, 1969)p. 6.
11. Itō Sei, *Bungei tokuhon*, in *Zenshū*, vol. 17, p. 156.
12. *Kokuminha* – the group of writers gathered round Tokutomi Sohō. Kunikida Doppo was one of the main contributors to Tokutomi's magazine *Kokumin no tomo*.
13. *Bungakukai* – a literary group gathered round the coterie magazine of the same name which appeared between 1893–8. The founder members included Shimazaki Tōson, Kitamura Tōkoku, Hoshino Tenchi, Ueda Bin and others. Among the contributors were Higuchi Ichiyō and Tayama Katai. Almost all members of *Bungakukai* were Christians at one time. Their main objective as a group was a search for the spiritual values of the West through studies of Western Renaissance romantic literature, and this made them quite distinct from *Ken'yūsha*.
14. Quoted in Yoshida Seiichi, *Gendai Nihon bungakushi* (Chikuma Shobo, 1965) p. 62.
15. Itō Sei, *Shōsetsu no hōhō*, p. 82.
16. Maruyama Masao, 'Patterns of Individuation', in M.B. Jansen (ed.), *Changing Attitudes*, p. 508.
17. Nakamura Mitsuo, *Modern Japanese Fiction*, vol. 1, pp. 7–8.
18. Ibid., p. 4.
19. Ibid., pp. 2–3.
20. Itō Sei, *Bungaku nyūmon*, in *Zenshū*, vol. 21, p. 317.
21. Itō Sei, *Shōsetsu no hōhō*, pp. 82–3.
22. Nakamura Mitsuo, *Modern Japanese Fiction*, vol. 1, p. 13.
23. Itō Sei, *Shōsetsu no hōhō*, p. 73.
24. Maruyama Masao, 'Patterns of Individuation', in M. B. Jansen (ed.), *Changing Attitudes*, p. 512.
25. Itō Sei, *Shōsetsu no hōhō*, p. 73.
26. Hirano Ken, 'Shishōsetsu niritsu haihan' (The Antinomy of the I-novel), in Hirano Ken, *Geijutsu to Jisseikatsu* (Shinchosha, 1964) pp. 17–19. This is an important article discussing the history and theory of the I-novel.
27. Itō Sei, *Shōsetsu no hōhō*, p. 72.
28. Ibid., pp. 74–5.
29. Ibid., pp. 63–4.
30. Nakamura Mitsuo, *Modern Japanese Fiction*, p. 5.
31. Itō Sei, *Shōsetsu no hōhō*, p. 74.

Notes to Chapter Three: From Flight to Self-destruction

1. For further discussion on the *shinkyō shōsetsu* see chapter 4.
2. Itō Sei, *Bungaku nyūmon*, in *Zenshū*, vol. 21, p. 330.

3. Yamamoto Kenkichi, *Shishōsetsu sakka ron* (Kadokawa Shoten, 1957).
4. Translated from Kasai Zenzō, *Ko o tsurete*, in *Nihon bungaku zenshū*, vol. 31 (Shueisha, 1969).
5. Itō Sei, 'Kindai Nihonjin no hassō no shokeishiki.' The quotation is taken from a partial translation of this essay entitled 'Modes of Thought in Contemporary Japan', *Japan Quarterly*, vol. 12 (1965) p. 508. All quotations from this article will be referred to hereafter as 'Modes of Thought', *JQ*.
6. Itō Sei, 'Modes of Thought', *JQ*, p. 511.
7. 'Logic of negation' is a term used by the historian Ienaga Saburō in his work *Nihon shisōshi ni okeru hitei ronri no hattatsu* (The Development of the Logic of Negation in the History of Japanese Thought), and with it Ienaga defines the categories of negation in Japanese Buddhism.
8. Katō Shūichi, *A History of Japanese Literature: The First Thousand Years* (Kodansha, 1979; London: Macmillan, 1979) p. 16.
9. Itō Sei, *Shōsetsu no hōhō*, p. 104.
10. See Itō Sei's work *Tōbō dorei to kamen shinshi*, in *Gendai bungaku taikei*, vol. 49 (Chikuma Shobo, 1965). The expression *kamen shinshi* is rather elliptical and 'gentleman in a mask' is only an approximate translation. It could equally denote someone hiding *behind* a 'gentleman's mask'.
11. Ibid., p. 400.
12. Itō Sei, *Shōsetsu no hōhō*, p. 102.
13. Itō Sei, 'Modes of Thought', *JQ*, p. 508.
14. The critics who developed the theory of histrionics in the I-novel are Hirano Ken, Itō Sei, Nakamura Mitsuo and Fukuda Tsuneari.
15. Itō Sei, *Honshitsu iten ron*, in *Zenshū*, vol. 17, pp. 46–50.
16. Hirano Ken, 'Shishōsetsu niritsu haihan', in *Geijutsu to Jisseikatsu*, p. 41.
17. Itō Sei, 'Modes of Thought', *JQ*, p. 509.
18. Ibid., p.509.
19. Fukuda Tsuneari, 'Kamura Isota', in *Fukuda Tsuneari hyōronshū*, vol. 13 (Shinchosha, 1966) p. 137.
20. Dazai Osamu, *Villon's Wife*, in D. Keene (ed.), *Modern Japanese Literature* (Tokyo: Charles E. Tuttle, 1957).
21. Dazai Osamu, *No Longer Human*; quoted by Minami Hiroshi, *Psychology of the Japanese People* (University of Tokyo Press, 1971) p. 71.
22. Itō Sei, *Bungaku nyūmon*, in *Zenshū*, vol. 21, p. 336.
23. Hirano Ken, 'Kamura Isota to Kasai Zenzō', in the introduction to *Nihon bungaku zenshū*, vol. 31. For further criticism of the feudal aspects of life in the *bundan* see chapters 6 and 7.
24. Itō Sei, *Shōsetsu no hōhō*, 111–12.

Notes to Chapter Four: In Search of Logic and Social Harmony

1. Itō Sei, *Shōsetsu no hōhō*, pp. 71–86.
2. Itō Sei, 'Modes of Thought', *JQ*, p. 503.
3. Ibid., p. 503.
4. Ibid., pp. 503–4.
5. Ibid., p. 504.
6. See above chapter 3.

7. Itō Sei, *Tōbō dorei to kamen shinshi*, in *Gendai bungaku taikei*, vol. 49, p. 399.

8. Itō Sei, *Shōsetsu no hōhō*, p. 201.

9. See his work *Fushinchū* (Under Construction, 1910).

10. Itō Sei, *Shōsetsu no hōhō*, p. 202.

11. Ibid., p. 203.

12. Ibid., p. 204.

13. Ibid., p. 204.

14. Itō Sei, 'Modes of Thought', *JQ*, p. 505.

15. Among the close associates of Natsume Sōseki were Nogami Toyoichirō, Nogami Yaeko, Terada Torahiko, Watsuji Tetsurō, Komiya Toyotaka, Akutagawa Ryūnosuke and Abe Jirō.

16. Even after Sōseki had made a name for himself as a professional writer, he kept up an abnormally high rate of production. He worked more than ordinary health could possibly bear, and early started suffering from severe stomach ulcers, which became the ultimate cause of his death at the age of fifty.

17. Itō Sei, 'Modes of Thought', *JQ*, pp. 504–9.

18. Maruyama Masao, *Nihon no shisō*, p. 74.

19. Itō Sei, 'Modes of Thought', *JQ*, p. 506.

20. Itō Sei, *Bungaku nyūmon*, in *Zenshū*, vol. 21, p. 348.

21. Itō Sei, 'Kindai nihonjin no hassō no shokeishiki', in *Gendai Nihon bungaku zenshū*, vol. 44 (Chikuma Shobo, 1955) pp. 285–6.

22. Arima Tatsuo, *The Failure of Freedom*, pp. 101–2.

23. Itō Sei, *Shōsetsu no hōhō*, p. 216.

24. Hirano Ken, 'Shishōsetsu niritsu haihan', in *Geijutsu to Jisseikatsu*, p. 21.

25. Itō Sei, *Shōsetsu no hoho*, p. 216.

26. Ibid., p. 217.

27. This process is fully discussed by Hirano Ken in *Waga sengo bungakushi*, in *Hirano Ken zenshū*, vol. 4 (Shinchosha, 1975) pp. 236–57.

28. Hirano Ken, 'Shishōsetsu niritsu haihan', in Hirano Ken, *Geijutsu to Jisseikatsu*, p. 26.

29. Translated by E. Seidensticker in D. Keene (ed.), *Modern Japanese Literature*.

30. Hirano Ken, 'Shishōsetsu niritsu haihan', in *Geijutsu to Jisseikatsu*, p. 28.

31. Itō Sei, *Bungaku nyūmon*, in *Zenshū*, vol. 21, pp. 365–73.

32. Itō Sei, *Honshitsu iten ron*, in *Zenshū*, vol. 17, pp. 47–50.

33. Itō Sei, *Bungaku nyūmon*, in *Zenshū*, vol. 21, p. 373.

34. Ibid., p. 374.

35. Tsurumi Shunsuke and Kuno Osamu, *Gendai Nihon no shisō* (Iwanami Shinsho, 1956) p. 9.

36. Itō Sei, *Shōsetsu no hōhō*, p. 217. Tsurumi Shunsuke, in Tsurumi Shunsuke and Kuno Osamu, *Gendai Nihon shisō*, pp. 14, 16, 28, writing about Mushanokōji's failure, points out two factors: the imperfect, disappointing human relations between the members of the village, and Mushanokōji's lack of understanding of the laws of capitalistic economics.

37. Itō Sei, *Shōsetsu no hōhō*, pp. 217–18.

38. Ibid.

39. Itō Sei, 'Kindai nihonjin no hassō no shokeishiki', in *Gendai Nihon bungaku zenshū*, vol. 44, p. 286.

40. Ibid.

41. Itō Sei considered the appearance of a writer like Miyamoto Yuriko to be part

of the natural development from the Taishō concept of individual harmony towards the Shōwa concept of social harmony. By contrast, Hirano Ken, for instance, felt that the gap between the concept of art in the Taishō and Shōwa periods, between the humanism of Shirakaba and the socially-engaged proletarian literature, was so deep, that the existence of Miyamoto Yuriko should be considered an exception rather than the rule in the development of Japanese literature (Hirano Ken, *Waga sengo bungakushi*, in *Hirano Ken zenshū*, vol. 4, p. 241).
42. Itō Sei, 'Modes of Thought', *JQ*, p. 507.

Notes to Chapter Five: In Search of Beauty

1. Itō Sei, 'Modes of Thought', *JQ*, p. 513.
2. Itō Sei, *Bungaku nyūmon*, in *Zenshū*, vol. 21, pp. 318–19.
3. The title *Uta andon* actually means a paper lantern, on which for decorative reasons a slip of paper with the text of a traditional *uta* (poem or song) is stuck.
4. Itō Sei, *Shōsetsu no hōhō*, p. 197.
5. Shinkankakuha, a literary movement formed by a group of writers, including Yokomitsu Riichi and Kawabata Yasunari, who gathered round the magazine *Bungei jidai* (founded in 1924).
6. Itō Sei, *Shōsetsu no hōhō*, p. 199.
7. Ibid., p. 198.
8. Ibid., p. 198.
9. Ibid., p. 200.
10. Ibid., p. 210.
11. Ibid., p. 210.
12. Itō Sei, *Bungaku nyūmon*, in *Zenshū*, vol. 21, p. 346.
13. Itō Sei, *Shōsetsu no hōhō*, p. 212.
14. Ibid., p. 209.
15. W. Norman (transl.), *Hell Screen*, in D. Keene (ed.), *Modern Japanese Literature*, p. 331.
16. Itō Sei, *Bungaku nyūmon*, in *Zenshū*, vol. 21, pp. 318–22.
17. Itō Sei, *Kindai Nihon no sakka no sōsaku hōhō*, in *Zenshū*, vol. 17, p. 165.
18. Ibid., pp. 160–1.
19. On the changing conditions in the *bundan* after the Russo-Japanese war, see chapter 2.
20. Itō Sei, *Kindai Nihon no sakka no sōsaku hōhō*, in *Zenshū*, vol. 17, p. 170.
21. See chapter 3.
22. Hirano Ken, *Waga sengo bungakushi*, in *Hirano Ken zenshū*, vol. 4, p. 203.
23. Ibid., p. 204.
24. Ibid., p. 204.
25. See for example Akagi Kōhei's article 'Yūtō bungaku no bokumetsu' (Eradication of the Literature of Dissipation, 1926). In the same article he criticised the works of both the naturalist I-novelist Chikamatsu Shūkō and of some aesthetic school writers like Goto Sueo and Kubota Mantarō. In his view both tended to pursue purely sensual effects, pampering to popular taste in a fashion not dissimilar to the pornographic type (*harubon*) of Edo period *gesaku* literature.

26. Nakamura Mitsuo, *Modern Japanese Fiction*, vol. 1, p. 11.
27. Itō Sei, *Shōsetsu no hōhō*, p. 207.
28. Ibid., p. 209.
29. Ibid., p. 205.
30. Katō Shūichi, 'Japanese Writers and Modernisation' in M. B. Jansen (ed.), *Changing Attitudes*, p. 432 n.
31. Itō Sei, *Shōsetsu no hōhō*, p. 206.
32. Ibid., p. 208.
33. Itō Sei, 'Kindai nihonjin no hassō no shokeishiki', in *Gendai Nihon bungaku zenshū*, vol. 44, p. 207.
34. E. Seidensticker, *Kafū the Scribbler* (Stanford, Cal.: Stanford University Press, 1965) p. 123.
35. Arima Tatsuo, *The Failure of Freedom*, p. 168.
36. Ibid., p. 153.
37. On the impact of the proletarian literary movement see chapter 6.
38. Itō Sei, 'Modes of Thought', *JQ*, p. 505.
39. Itō Sei, *Shōsetsu no hōhō*, p. 212.
40. Ibid., p. 213–14.
41. Ibid., p. 214.

Notes to Chapter Six: The Revolutionary Ideal

1. Itō Sei, 'Kindai nihonjin no hassō no shokeishiki', in *Gendai Nihon bungaku zenshū*, vol. 44, p. 296.
2. Maruyama Masao, 'Patterns of Individuation' in M. B. Jansen (ed.), *Changing Attitudes*, p. 521.
3. Arima Tatsuo, *The Failure of Freedom*, p. 175.
4. Ibid., p. 176.
5. Quoted in Maruyama Masao, *Nihon no shisō*, p. 81.
6. Itō Sei, *Shōsetsu no hōhō*, p. 103.
7. Maruyama Masao, *Nihon no shisō*, p. 81.
8. Ibid., p. 75.
9. Maruyama Masao, 'Patterns of Individuation' in M. B. Jansen (ed.), *Changing Attitudes*, p. 522.
10. Arima Tatsuo, *The Failure of Freedom*, p. 179.
11. Itō Sei, *Tōbō dorei to kamen shinshi*, in *Gendai bungaku taikei*, vol. 49, p. 399.
12. Hirano Ken, 'Kobayashi Takiji to puroretaria bungaku', in *Nihon no kindai bungaku* (Yomiuri Shinbunsha, 1964) p. 233.
13. Hirano Ken, *Bungaku–Shōwa jūnen zengo*, in *Hirano Ken zenshū*, vol. 4, pp. 428–9.
14. Itō Sei, *Shōsetsu no hōhō*, p. 109.
15. The concept of harmony rather than open conflict was also a central feature of the legal system, and every effort was made by conciliators to prevent cases from coming into court. See J. George, 'Law in Modern Japan', in J. H. Hall and R. K. Beardsley, *Twelve Doors to Japan* (New York: McGraw-Hill, 1965) p. 494.
16. Itō Sei, 'Kindai nihonjin no hassō no shokeishiki', in *Gendai Nihon bungaku zenshū*, vol. 44, p. 289.
17. Minami Hiroshi, *Psychology of the Japanese People*, p. 71.

18. Itō Sei, 'Kindai nihonjin no hassō no shokeishiki', in *Gendai Nihon bungaku zenshū*, vol. 44, p. 289.
19. Itō Sei, *Shōsetsu no hōhō*, p. 132.
20. Ibid., p. 133.

Notes to Chapter Seven: Decline

1. Maruyama Masao, 'Patterns of Individuation', in M. B. Jansen (ed.), *Changing Attitudes*, p. 517.
2. Ibid., p. 517.
3. Ibid., p. 518.
4. Ibid., p. 518.
5. Quoted in Hirano Ken, *Bungaku – Shōwa jūnen zengo*, in *Hirano Ken zenshū*, vol. 4, p. 415.
6. Ibid., p. 420.
7. Itō Sei, 'Kindai nihonjin no hassō no shokeishiki', in *Gendai Nihon bungaku zenshū*, vol. 44, p. 288.
8. Itō Sei, *Kyūdosha to ninshikisha* (Shinchosha, 1962) p. 169.
9. *Shuppan kinenkai* – a party commemorating publication of a work by a new author, given by his literary friends and elders.
10. Oya Sōichi, 'Bundan girudo no kaitaiki', in *Shōwa hihyō taikei*, vol. 1 (Bancho Shobo, 1974) pp. 348–52.
11. Itō Sei, 'Kindai nihonjin no hassō no shokeishiki', in *Gendai Nihon bungaku zenshū*, vol. 44, p. 290.
12. Itō Sei, is considered by Hirano Ken to be a writer who broke the deadlock of the I-novel by introducing Western methods of objectivity and psychological analysis into the description of the 'I'. Due to Itō Sei's efforts the Western literary method was firmly rooted in modern Japanese literature.
13. Itō Sei, 'Kindai nihonjin no hassō no shokeishiki', in *Gendai Nihon bungaku zenshū*, vol. 44, p. 291.
14. Maruyama Masao, 'Patterns of Individuation', in M. B. Jansen (ed.), *Changing Attitudes*, pp. 496–531.
15. Ibid.
16. Hirano Ken (*Waga sengo bungakushi*, in *Hirano Ken zenshū*, vol. 4, p. 234) suggests that the attitude of histrionic self-destruction that characterised Dazai's life and work, was partly an effect of his deeply-felt personal failure in the revolutionary movement. In this sense a work like *Dōke no hana* could be read as a variant on *tenkō bungaku*. Takami Jun's *Kokyū wasureubeki* and Dazai's *Dōke no hana* give, in different ways, expression to the same spirit of conversion.
17. B. Crick, *In Defence of Politics* (Harmondsworth: Penguin Books, 1964) p. 40.
18. Hidaka Rokuro, '*Bundan to jarunarizumu*' in *Bungaku Iwanami kōza*, vol. 2 (Iwanami, 1952).
19. Togaeri Hajime, '"Bundan" hokai ron', in *Shōwa hihyō taikei*, vol. 4, (Bancho Shobo, 1974) pp. 84–5.
20. Ibid.
21. Itō Sei, *Soshiki to ningen*, in *Zenshū*, vol. 17, pp. 137–8.
22. Ibid., p. 139.
23. Ibid., p. 141.

Bibliography

Japanese Sources
Ara Masahito, *Shimin bungakuron* (Tokyo: K. K. Aoki Shoten, 1955).
Arima Tatsuo, *The Failure of Freedom: A Portrait of Modern Japanese Intellectuals* (Cambridge, Mass.: Harvard University Press, 1969).
Chie Nakane *Japanese Society* (London: Weidenfeld and Nicolson, 1970).
Doi Takeo, *The Anatomy of Dependence* (Tokyo: Kodansha, 1977).
Fukuda Tsuneari, *Fukuda Tsuneari hyōronshū* (Tokyo: Shinchosha, 1966).
Fukutake Tadashi, *Man and Society in Japan* (University of Tokyo Press, 1962).
Hirano Ken, *Hirano Ken zenshū* (Tokyo: Shinchosha, 1975), in particular vols 1, 2, 4 and 6.
——, Odagiri Hideo and Yamamoto Kenkichi (eds), *Gendai Nihon bungaku ronsōshi* (Tokyo: Miraisha, 1956).
Hirotsu Kazuo, *Nengetsu no ashioto* (Tokyo: Kodansha, 1969).
Honda Shūgo, *Monogatari sengo bungakushi* (Tokyo: Shinchosha, 1965).
Itō Sei (ed.), *Bungaku Iwanami kōza* (Tokyo: Iwanami Shoten, 1952).
——, *Itō Sei zenshū* (Tokyo: Shinchosha, 1973), in particular vols 16–18, 21.
——, *Nihon bundanshi* (Tokyo: Kodansha, 1979), contains 24 volumes of which the first 18 were written by Itō Sei himself, and the remaining six by his close friend and co-operator Senuma Shigeki after Itō Sei's death.
Kamei Hideo, *Itō Sei no sekai* (Tokyo: Kodansha, 1969).
Karaki Junzō, *Muyōmono no keifu* (Tokyo: Chikuma Shobo, 1964).
Kindai Nihon Bungakkan (ed.), *Nihon no kindai bungaku: hito to sakuhin* (Tokyo: Yomiuri Shinbunsha 1964).
Kōsaka Masaaki, *Japanese Thought in the Meiji Era* (Tokyo: Pan-Pacific Press, 1958).
Maruyama Masao, *Thought and Behaviour in Modern Japanese Politics* (Oxford University Press, 1963).
——, *Nihon no shisō* (Tokyo: Iwanami Shinsho, 1961).
Minami Hiroshi, *Psychology of the Japanese People* (University of Tokyo Press, 1971).
Muramatsu Takeshi, Saeki Shōichi and Okubo Norio (eds), *Shōwa hihyō taikei* (Tokyo: Bancho Shobo, 1974).
Nakamura Mitsuo, *Fūzoku shōsetsuron* (Tokyo: Kawade Shobo, 1954).
——, *Modern Japanese Fiction* (Tokyo: Kokusai Bunka Shinkokai, 1968).
Nakamura Shinichirō, *Kono hyakunen no shōsetsu* (Tokyo: Shinchosha, 1974).
Odagiri Hideo, *Bungakushi* (Tokyo: Toyo Keizai Shinposha, 1961).
——, *Gendai Nihon no sakkatachi* (Tokyo: Hosei University Press, 1962).
Okazaki Yoshie, *Japanese Literature in the Meiji Era* (Tokyo: Obunsha, 1955).
Okubo Fusao, *Bunshi to bundan* (Tokyo: Kodansha, 1970).

Shuichi Kato, *A History of Japanese Literature: The First Thousand Years* (London: Macmillan, 1979; Tokyo: Kodansha, 1979).

Tsurumi Shunsuke and Kuno Osamu, *Gendai Nihon shisō* (Tokyo: Iwanami Shinsho, 1956).

Yoshida Seiichi, *Gendai Nihon bungakushi* (Tokyo: Chikuma Shobo, 1965).

Westerm Sources

Albrecht, Milton C., Barnett, James H., and Griff, Meson (eds.), *The Sociology of Art and Literature: A Reader* (London: Gerald Duckworth, 1970).

Berger, Peter L., *Invitation to Sociology: A Humanistic Perspective* (Harmondsworth: Penguin Books, 1966).

Bottomore, E., *Elites and Society* (London: C. A. Watts, 1964).

Bradbury, Malcolm, *The Social Context of Modern English Literature* (Oxford: Basil Blackwell, 1971).

Coser, L., *Men of Ideas: A Sociologist's View* (New York: Free Press, 1965).

Crick, Bernard, *In Defence of Politics* (Harmondsworth: Penguin Books, 1964).

Dore, R. P., *Aspects of Social Change in Modern Japan* (Princeton University Press, 1967).

Hall, J. H., and Beardsley, R. K., *Twelve Doors to Japan* (New York: McGraw-Hill, 1965).

Jansen, Marius B. (ed.), *Changing Japanese Attitudes toward Modernisation* (Princeton University Press, 1969).

Keene, D., *World within Walls* (London: Secker & Warburg, 1976).

—— (ed.), *Modern Japanese Literature* (Tokyo: Charles E. Tuttle, 1957).

Lifton, R., Kato, S., and Reich, R., *Six Lives, Six Deaths: Portraits from Modern Japan* (London: Yale University Press, 1979).

Pyle, K., *The New Generation in Meiji Japan: Problems of Cultural Identity 1885–1895* (Stanford University Press, 1969).

Ryan, M., *Japan's First Modern Novel* (New York: Columbia University Press, 1967).

Morris, I. (ed.), *Modern Japanese Stories* (Tokyo: Charles E. Tuttle, 1962).

Sansom, G., *The Western World and Japan* (New York: Cresset Press, 1950).

Seidensticker, E., *Kafū the Scribbler* (Stanford University Press, 1965).

Shively, D. H. (ed.), *Tradition and Modernisation in Japanese Culture* (Princeton University Press, 1971).

Sibley, W. F., *The Shiga Hero* (University of Chicago Press, 1979).

Ward, Robert E. (ed.), *Political Development in Modern Japan* (Princeton University Press, 1968).

—— (ed.), *Political Modernisation in Japan and Turkey* (Princeton University Press, 1964).

Wellek, R., and Warren, A., *Theory of Literature* (Harmondsworth: Penguin Books, 1978).

Williams, Raymond, *The Long Revolution* (New York: Harper & Row, 1966).

——, *Culture and Society 1780–1950* (Harmondsworth: Penguin Books, 1961).

Index

定価5,000円
in Japan